PROJECT MANAGEMENT:

Meeting Project Auditors' and Reviewers' Expectations - No Spot!

A Practical Guide for Project Managers, Auditors, and Reviewers

Osondu Joshua Onwuzuruigbo

PROJECT MANAGEMENT:
Meeting Project Auditors' and Reviewers' Expectations – No Spot!

ISBN: 978-978-68-5749-7 (Print)
ISBN: 978-978-68-5750-3 (Ebook)

Published and Printed by:
Cheret Creative Company
Terebinth, 13, Alice Fatumo Idowu Street, Oluwo-kekere, Bashorun, Ibadan, Nigeria
T: +234 803 095 7661
E: hello@cheretcreatives.com, cheretcreativecompany@gmail.com
W: www.cheretcreatives.com
Facebook/Twitter/Instagram/LinkedIn/Google: @CheretCreatives

The Author can be reached at: jo_andc@yahoo.com; +234 803 341 4727
Cover Design: AkinWaleEkunDayo

First print: 2026

Text set in Arno Pro and Titillium Web Pro.
Printed in the Federal Republic of Nigeria

ENDORSEMENTS

Drawing from decades of experience managing development projects that passed audits by most of the key international audit firms, Onwuzuruigbo Joshua Osondu delivers an essential guide for project management teams working on projects funded by Multilateral Development Banks and International Financing Institutions. This book transforms the dreaded audit process from a source of anxiety into an opportunity for excellence by revealing exactly what auditors and reviewers look for during financial and performance assessments. Rather than a traditional project management textbook, it serves as a strategic preparation manual that will enable project teams to confidently demonstrate best practices in financial management, procurement, contract administration, and risk management.

Dr. Shamsuddeen Usman, CON, OFR
Former Nigeria Minister of Finance (2007 – 2009) and Minister of National Planning (2009 – 2013)

This authoritative and practice-driven book lifts the veil on project audits and reviews, clearly revealing what auditors expect and how project teams can consistently achieve outstanding ratings with confidence. Grounded in real-world experience from multilateral and development-financed projects, it is a must-have guide for project managers, auditors, reviewers, development partners seeking excellence, credibility and success in project delivery as well as scholars in higher educational institutions.

Professor Azikiwe Peter Onwualu, FAS
President, African University of Science and Technology, Abuja

---

AKNOWLEDGEMENTS

BEGINNING MY CAREER, Mr. Martins Akumazi assiduously mentored me enabling my later strength in quantity surveying and project management. I will like to sincerely thank him. My appreciation also goes to Dr. Karl Voltaire who trusted my capacity and entrusted the management of all the projects being supported by international development agencies then at the Nelson Mandela Institution and African University of Science and Technology (AUST), Abuja to me. At the time of managing those projects, Dr. Olajide Babatunde was there to provide oversight function that led to the success of the projects. I also sincerely thank him. Even though I have Finance background, I am not an Accountant. Two excellent professional accountants whom I very much drew tremendous knowledge from while they were in my project management team at AUST and Association of African University, Accra, Ghana are Benjamin Okonkwo and Frank Adjei respectively. Our working together in unity have contributed to the so much technical guidance that I have provided in this book as regards to financial audits and financial management in general. I am grateful to you both.

Finally, I cannot quantify the confidence that I had gained while finalizing the book when I received the comment of one of the outstanding former Ministers of Finance and Ministers of National Planning in Nigeria, Dr. Shamsuddeen Usman saying that after scanning through the book, he finds it interesting. This exceptionally encouraged me to complete the book knowing that it would sure serve its intended purpose. I am very grateful to you, sir. Furthermore, I sincerely appreciate Dr. Tunde Adekola and Prof. Peter Azikiwe Onwualu respectively for accepting to write the Foreward and Blurb to this book. I sincerely thank my friend who is one of the finest Virtual Artists in Africa, John Adeleye Aderinkomi for undertaking the design of the Back-Cover of this book at no cost to me.

In conclusion, my earnest appreciations go to my wife, Blessing and children - Mishael, Tehila and Onyinyechi, all of who granted me great support and were patient with me while I use their rightfully deserved time of companionship to put together this book. Above all and ultimately, I am totally grateful to God Almighty for empowering me and making the creation of this book possible.

TABLE OF CONTENTS

LIST OF FIGURES

LIST OF TABLES

ABBREVIATIONS

1. ACWP: Actual Cost of Work Performed
2. AIN: Actual Inflow
3. AP: Advance Payment
4. BAC: Budget at Completion
5. BAFO: Best and Final Offer
6. BCWP: Budgeted Cost of Work Performed
7. BCWS: Budgeted Cost of Work Schedule
8. COSO: Committee of Sponsoring Organizations of the Treadway Report
9. EAC: Estimate at Completion
10. GAAS: Generally Accepted Auditing Standards
11. GAGAS: Generally Accepted Governmental Auditing Standards
12. IFRS: International Financial Reporting Standards
13. ISA: International Standards on Auditing
14. LC: Letter of Credit
15. LCS: Least Cost-based Selection
16. PCAOB: Public Company Accounting Oversight Board
17. PIN: Planned Inflow
18. QBS: Quality-based Selection
19. QCBS: Quality and Cost-based Selection
20. RMF: Result Measurement Framework

21. SAS: Statement on Auditing Standards
22. SMART: Specific, Measurable, Achievable, Relevant, and Time-bound
23. UN: United Nations
24. UNESCAP: United Nations Economic and Social Commission for Asia and the Pacific
25. WBG: World Bank Group
26. WBS: Work Breakdown Structure

FOREWORD

I AM HONORED TO INTRODUCE *"Project Management: Meeting Project Auditors' and Reviewers' Expectations – No Spot!"* by Osondu J. Onwuzuruigbo. In my former role as a Senior Education Specialist and Task Team member at the World Bank, I participated severally in supervision missions and review teams at different stages in the life cycle of numerous projects. A common observation during these engagements was that many project implementation teams lacked confidence in their project management practices. Consequently, they were often uncertain whether they would be commended or sanctioned during review missions. This uncertainty frequently resulted in anxiety and, at times, revealed either capacity gaps or a lack of clear understanding of what is required to satisfy auditors and reviewers beyond reasonable doubt that a project is on track for success.

This book builds on project management fundamentals and best practices to provide project managers—particularly those responsible for projects supported by development agencies—with clear insights into the expectations of auditors and reviewers. It proposes practical approaches that not only meet these expectations but also promote the openness, transparency, and accountability necessary for achieving project objectives. Conversely, reviewers engaged in project assessments often focus narrowly on areas aligned with the core deliverables of the project, while overlooking the project management dimension, which is in fact the key driver of successful implementation. This book highlights these gaps for the attention of project auditors, reviewers, and Independent Verification Agents (IVAs), thereby ensuring a comprehensive, results-oriented review process that ultimately benefits the project.

The author's background in quantity surveying and finance, his extensive experience in project management, and his numerous high-level interactions with top-rated international financial management and audit firms—interactions that consistently concluded without adverse findings—form the solid foundation of this book. The text is well written, concise, and highly relevant, as it clearly elucidates both operational and non-operational aspects of project management. These include compliance, planning, budgeting, staffing, coordination, procurement, contract management, financial management, auditing, disbursement, reporting, and governance. In essence, the book equips project managers to withstand rigorous reviews and enables reviewers to conduct impact-driven, comprehensive project assessments. It addresses critical audit dimensions, including financial, performance, fiduciary, risk management, and governance audits.

Given its content and approach, this book is clearly multifaceted in scope and audience. I therefore strongly recommend it to state and non-state actors at national, state, and local levels; relevant Ministries, Departments, and Agencies

(MDAs); public and private sector organizations; multilateral and bilateral development partners; non-governmental and civil society organizations; as well as academic, technical, and professional associations. Its adoption will significantly contribute to improved project delivery—without spots.

Dr. Tunde Adekola

Former Senior Education Specialist, World Bank

PREFACE

What this book is about?

This book is not a primary book for project management. However, it provides the basis for testing the project management performance of persons or teams entrusted with the responsibility of carrying out the day-to-day management of the project with the aim of leading the project to a successful end. Success here relates to completion of the project within allocated time period and budgeted cost, and at best specifications of the deliverables, with minimal changes to scope, cost and quality.

This book is about, firstly, getting the project management team know that someone will sometime in the future assess how it has carried out its management functions of planning, organizing, staffing, directing and controlling, towards the accomplishment of the project's objectives. Secondly, the book is about having the project management team informed of the interest areas and would-be focus of auditors and reviewers during audits or reviews of its projects. And, thirdly, the book is about the essential preparations that the project management team ought to make in order not to fall short of the auditors' or reviewers' expectations of an excellent project management poised to achieving successful completion of the project. Projects referred to in this book are particularly those funded by Multilateral Development Banks and International Financing Institutions. However, as such projects epitomize best practice; the preparations expected from the project management team here can be adopted for all projects.

The need for the book

Most times the outcome and consequences of an audit or review of a project determine the basis of the continuation or otherwise of both the project and the project management team. As it may seem like the fate of the project management team lies on the outcome, the conduct of audits or reviews on its project is dreaded by most project management teams. There is lack of confidence on the part of the team just because they do not know the exact things the auditors or reviewers will be looking out for and so they are not certain whether the outcome will be favorable – attract commendation, or adverse – attract sanction. The consideration that the purpose of audit or review of the project includes helping to improve the performance of the project and project management team is thrown into the air. This could lead to misbehavior of the project management team before or at the time of the audit or review. This ought not be so. This book unveils to the project management team the expectations of the auditors or reviewers and helps to get them make preparations accordingly and be confident.

Through these preparations by the project management team in anticipation of the auditors or reviewers, and by mere working towards satisfying them when they do arrive to conduct the audit or review, the project management team would have by default be performing its project management functions creditably. After all, it is not in anyone's interest – the project financiers, government and beneficiaries to see both or either the project management team or the project fails due to poor project management.

Another aspect of the need for this book concerns the auditors and reviewers engaged to carry out audit or review exercise on projects. While most financial auditors so engaged are properly equipped in view of the accounting profession they are of, it is not exactly same for some of them and most reviewers. While financial audits are predominantly on businesses and not on projects, most of the reviewers employed to carry out the review exercise, though may be experts in the core subject of the project do not have sufficient requisite knowledge of project management. This makes it impossible to effectively review and report on the most critical element of the project delivery process, project management, as they do not know exactly what ought to be the focus. This book provides to the reviewers a guide to effective assessment of the projects and proper reporting covering essential information for appropriate decisions by the relevant stakeholders. For those financial auditors that are not conversant with financial audit of projects, the book will also equip them with ease for such assignments.

The scope of the book

In equipping the project management team and positioning it to excel during the most critical and frequent audit, financial audit, this book in detail but with simplicity for the understanding of the team covers financial audit related issues that include:

- Purpose of Financial Audit;
- Financial Statement;
- Internal Control;
- Basis of Auditor's Opinion;
- Audit Process;
- Auditor's Areas of Interest;
- Auditor's Opinion;
- Reporting Structure of the Observed Weaknesses; and
- Measures to Satisfy the Auditor

The larger proportion of this book deals with Performance Audit which is an independent assessment of the project to determine firstly the achievements of the defined project's objectives reflected by the inputs, outputs, results and impacts, and secondly the efficiency, economy and effectiveness of the operations in attaining the achievements. The purpose, process and basis of the assessment are discussed. Above all, with the aim of positioning the project and the project management team for high performance rating, this book provides best practices for core elements of project management which also are likely to be the focus of the reviewers as in the event of poor handling of these parts of project management will lead to poor performance of the project. The considered elements are Work Plan; Budget; Procurements of Goods, Works and Service; Contract Management; and Cash Flow Management. The discussion on each of these covers the concept; preparation and administration of relevant and related documents; and reviewer's areas of concentration and basis of assessment.

The key criteria for the assessment of the project management team's compliance with fiduciary requirements is another aspect of this book. The subjects of the fiduciary responsibilities discussed include: Financing Agreement; Financial Management; Procurement and Contract Management; Project Management Reports; Records Management; and Anti-Corruption. The book concentrated more on Financial Management of which the project management team in order to have a positive outlook need to be grounded on what is expected of them from the reviewers. Basic components of Financial Management in connection with projects discussed include: Fund Flow; Work Planning and Budget; Internal Control; Accounting and Financial Reporting; Internal and External Audits; and Disbursements among others.

Risks are crucial to the realization of project's objective and therefore form an important element of consideration during reviews. This book equips the project management team in this regard as it discusses risk management process – the creation, adoption and operationalization of the process. It further considers what constitutes effective and efficient risk management and how risk management documents can be employed for this purpose.

Finally, as project governance is critical to the success of the project, this book covers the subject, identifying its characteristics and functions for better project performance. The roles that the project management team can play to catalyze the activeness of the project governance body are also outlined in the book.

Intended Audience

The primary audience this book is intended to serve are

project managers and members of project management teams, otherwise recognized as Project Implementation Units for projects funded by Multilateral Development Banks and International Financing Institutions. It can also suitably serve those project managers and management teams involved in other projects. Financial Auditors and Reviewers of varied backgrounds employed to carry out financial audits or reviews respectively of projects will find this book useful. As it will be of interest to the development agencies or sponsors of project to see that both the project management teams and reviewers engaged in their projects are well equipped to excellently perform their respective assignments, this book will be helpful to these financiers in formulating guides for the purpose. This book will appeal to accounting students in the subject of financial audit particularly as it relates to projects.

Also, students of project management program that look forward to getting involved in large projects that are reasonably independent, beyond the traditional internally located projects in organizations, will find this book appealing. Other students in related management programs such as business management, MBA and construction management will also benefit from this book. Lecturers and academic researchers may also find the book useful. Finally, but not the least, practitioners such as quantity surveyors, engineers and architects involved in capital and infrastructure projects will indeed find this book very useful in the management of projects.

CHAPTER ONE

INTRODUCTION

Purpose of This Book

THE PURPOSE OF THIS BOOK is in two folds.

First is to have the project management team informed of the likely focus of auditors and reviewers during the conduct of audits and reviews on the project and to prepare the team on the measures to take to meet the goodly expectations of the auditors and reviewers. By knowing the need of and seeking to satisfy the auditors, the project management team by default pursues excellent project management.

Second purpose, is to provide a guide to the reviewers on what should be the focus of the assessment during reviews particularly as it concerns project management that is critical to the success of the project.

The Project

There are many definitions of a project but one that seems encompassing yet apt provides as follows:

> *"an endeavour in which human, material and financial resources are organized in a novel way, to undertake a unique scope of work of given specification, within constraints of cost and time, so as to achieve unitary, beneficial change, through the delivery of quantified and qualitative objectives."*
>
> – **C. Chapman and Stephen Ward,** 2010: Turner, 1992

Based on the above definition, some of the facts that make a project distinct from normal business endeavors in perpetuity are that:

- It has a measurable and specific objectives and goals;
- It has a definite start and end dates;
- The funding has a known limit;
- The objectives and goals when achieved creates measurable value - deliverables;
- The required human and material resources are obtained for the purpose of creating the values

To understand better, simple characteristics of a project is that it has three essential components, namely scope, budget and schedule. Scope components contain the deliverables with the associated specifications; budget has the cost limit; and schedule, the time limit. Connecting these components, according to **G. Oberiender, 2014**, is quality which also is an integral part of each of the components.

Beyond these traditional characteristics, a project is also viewed from the perspective of its domiciliation and control. **Bekker, 2015** attempting to define project governance has provided three classifications of projects in this regard. The first classification is where the project is located in an organization as such that it is part of and not independent of that organization, the parent organization. The operation of such project is ruled by the internal mechanism of the organization in which case the project governance is exercised within the structure of the organization and involves the control, management, supervision and monitoring of the project by the organization's management. Most projects in the private sector particularly where the size is small and the completion period is short are in this category.

The second classification of projects is where there are two or more organizations participating in the project in which case the control, management, supervision and monitoring of the project are based on the relationships, agreement, collaborations and contracts among the organizations.

The third classification is where the project is considered a temporary organization. In this case, the control, management, supervision and monitoring of the project is endogenous to the project with only the project governance external. Projects that fall into this category are mostly those that are long-term, and complex, large in size, and have the resources deployed almost full-time. A very large number of projects that are in the public sector and funded by Multilateral Development Banks and International Financing Institutions are in this classification of projects. The implementation of such projects is usually carried out by the Project Implementation Units, fully or quasi-independent entity established for the purpose. The project as referred to in this book is exclusively the projects in this classification that are funded by Multilateral Development Banks and International Financing Institutions. The project management team constitutes the Project Implementation Unit responsible for the management of the project.

Project Management Team

The project management team as used in this book represents the Project Implementation Unit generally, and in some sense the project manager. The project management team having been established for the purpose of realizing the project's objectives undertakes the day-to-day management of the project. In this regard, the project management team has a common goal and shared responsibilities to carry out the project management as such to actualize the project in terms of scope, cost and time. This role of the project management team makes both the establishment and performance of the team a fundamental consideration for the owners, financiers, and beneficiaries of the project as they gaze at the project's expected end.

A typical project management team will have people of diverse but relevant expertise and experiences in order to drive the project to a successful completion. Some of the common expertise in most projects funded by Multilateral Development Banks and International Financing Institutions forthwith referred as development agencies are procurement expert, accountant, internal auditor, monitoring and evaluation expert, etc. Other expertise that may be involved are dependent on the nature, size, complexity, peculiarity and activities of the project.

Each member of the team with a defined expertise and role is expected to contribute to the effectiveness of the team towards delivering the project. This should be done based on the four principles of effective team as opined by **A. Joseph and B. Rubenstein, 2018** namely: accountability, transparency, integrity, and commitment. Just as each member is bound in his responsibilities to the team on these bases, the team functioning as the agents of the owner (government), financiers (development agencies), and beneficiaries (public) of the project are also bound in its responsibilities of project management necessary to actualize and make the project a success. Success here relates to completion of the project within allocated time period and budgeted cost, and at best specifications of the deliverables, with minimal changes to scope, cost and quality.

Project Management

Project management is a unique form of management as rather than normal functional management where management function is vertical along a single discipline or business. It involves coordination and management of resources horizontally across different functional lines or disciplines. The function of project management usually rests on an individual, the project manager. However, in this book, the project management team formed through a pool of personnel from functional lines (ministries, departments, or agencies of governments, and/or private sector) is considered as collectively undertaking the function.

Project management is the art and science of coordinating resources (people, materials, funds, equipment, facilities, technology, goodwill, etc.) in an economic, effective, and efficient manner to complete the project within allocated time period and budgeted cost, and at best specifications of the deliverables, with minimal changes to scope, cost and quality.

As with all management, these art and science involve five functions: planning, organizing, staffing, directing, and controlling. How these functions are carried out is a critical determinant of how successful the project can be. The project management team having been established not only accepts to undertake these functions but impliedly gives an assurance that it has the required expertise, and will exercise professionalism, high standard of ethics, diligence, and commitment towards successful completion of the project. As an agent, it will be imprudent on its part to care less, and assume that the principals also will do same concerning its quality of performance of these duties. In view that project generally involves large investments and high risks, there will always be a continuous interest of the principals – financiers, government and beneficiaries to check on the project management to ensure that the realization of the project's objectives reasonably remains secured. This check may be in various forms but mostly is undertaken through the engagement of auditors, reviewers, evaluators, etc.

The Auditors

The term audit is normally associated with financial audit that involves an independent examination and evaluation of the financial statements of an organization to ascertain and express an opinion on its trueness with respect to the observed transactions and financial records. The auditor is the one that is engaged and given the authority to carry out this duty with all honesty, and advise the external body exercising governance oversight on the organization. This duty as always involves verification of the information provided by the management of the organization and review of its performance regarding management and accountability of the financial resources entrusted to it. For our purpose in this book, the organization is the project and the management, the project management team.

In projects, examination of operations, verification of information, reviews of the discharge of assigned duties and expression of opinion on all are not only done over the project by an independent person with respect to financial resources but other areas of responsibilities of the project management team. In this book, the term audit has been applied generically to include the conduct of these exercises on the key areas of responsibilities of project management team for development agencies' funded projects. So, a wider use of the person, auditor has been adopted and sometimes interchangeably used as reviewers.

The areas of audit covered in this book are:

- Financial Audit;
- Performance Audit;
- Fiduciary Audit;
- Risk Audit; and
- Governance Audit.

Arrangement of This Book

The most critical and regularly externally conducted exercise on project is financial audit. Unfortunately, it is the most dreaded exercise that project management team looks forward to. Moreover, the outcome and consequences of financial audit determine the basis of the continuation or otherwise of both the project and the management team. Therefore, this book in its first main Chapters, Chapter 2 deals with Financial Audit. It positions the project manager and his team to understand the purpose of financial audit; have an in roll into the process the audit may follow; appreciate the determinants and nature of auditor's opinion; and make preparations that guarantee auditor's affirmation of both the project and the management team.

Chapter 3, Performance Audit, presents one of the audits

that a project is not likely to escape in its life-cycle. It may come up once or severally during the initiation, planning, execution or after completion of the project. Just as in financial audit, fundamental decisions of 'go-stop' are taken by the financiers based on the outcome of this audit. The purpose of performance audit is to determine firstly the achievements of the defined project's objectives reflected by the inputs, outputs, results and impacts, and secondly the efficiency, economy and effectiveness of the operations in attaining the achievements. Therefore, the Chapter informs and indeed guides the project management team on major tools and elements of project management that the team will need to pay much attention to and focus on as these are poised to contributing to favorable performance audit outcome in the future. They include:

- Work Plan;
- Budget;
- Procurement of Works, Goods, and Services;
- Contract Management;
- Cash Flow Management

Compliance on the part of the project management team with the fiduciary requirements of the project is another area of audit. Chapter 4, Fiduciary Audit, provides the project management team with a clearer understanding of the constituents of fiduciary requirements associated with development agencies' funded projects. Additionally, it discusses the control risks areas that the reviewer will focus on in the course of the assessment which also the project management team need be conscious of. These include:

- Financing Agreement;

- Financial Management:
  - Project Management Team Capacity;
  - Fund Flow;
  - Work Planning and Budget;
  - Internal Control;
  - Accounting and Financial Reporting;
  - Internal Audit;
  - External Audit;
  - Disbursement; and
  - Counterpart Fund
- Procurement and Contract Management;
- Project Management Reports;
- Records Management; and
- Anti-Corruption

Beyond the financial, performance, and fiduciary audits which risks are integral part of, Chapter 5, Risk Audit, deals comprehensively with the assessment of the project management team's consideration and treatment of risks, both financial and operational. The Chapter teaches the team risk management processes which also are the focus of the audit in view of its impact on the outcomes of projects.

Finally, although project governance is not an area of responsibility of the project management team, a global review of the project includes an assessment of project governance. This is necessary to assure the financiers that the project governance function is causing the project to move or remain in the right direction with the right speed and cost. Chapter 6, Governance Audit, presents the functions and other issues of project governance that the project management team need be aware of, pay attention to, thus can strategically aid the fulfillment of what is expected of the project's governance bodies.

CHAPTER TWO

FINANCIAL AUDIT

AMONG THE AUDITS that a project will be subjected to during its life cycle and beyond is financial audit. Financial audits are categorized into two namely, internal audit and external audit but for our discussion, we will concentrate on external audit. However, it is important to first distinguish the two particularly in terms of the role each plays on the project. Generally, while the external auditor on annual basis adopts a shortcut to the verification of accounting information contained in the annual financial statements of the project, the internal auditor is resident and keeps an eye on the employment and utilization of the resources that will later become part of the financial statements.

INTERNAL AUDIT

The Institute of Internal Auditors, 2017 defines internal auditing as follows:

> *Internal auditing is an independent, objective assurance and consulting activity designed to add value and improve an organization's operations. It helps an organization accomplish its objectives by bringing a systematic, disciplined approach to evaluate and improve the effectiveness of risk management, control, and governance processes.*

In a simple term, internal auditing focuses on facilitating the operations and financial management of the project to guarantee the effectiveness, efficiency, and economy (i.e. value-for-money) and ensuring that the functionaries have strong regard to compliance with contracts, laws and regulations without neglecting ethics and values.

To achieve these enormous tasks, the internal auditor is seen not only causing the strict implementation of the internal control in place but also always reviewing same and evaluating the strength and weaknesses in order to instill the necessary adjustments towards the realization of the project goals.

Although the internal audit unit is part of the project execution, it is autonomous and functions independently to fulfil the desired objective. In order words, its activities are not controlled by the internal structure of the project but by the external governance body to which it reports to.

At the end of each round of audit which is more frequent than that of the external auditor, the internal auditor produces reports that are submitted to the governance entities external to the project management team. The report will usually contain observations and recommendations which the authority reviews and approve as appropriate. It is the duty of the internal auditor to ensure that his approved recommendations are implemented in the project's management going forward.

EXTERNAL AUDIT

Most times the outcome and consequences of this audit determine the basis of the continuation or otherwise of both the project and the management team. It is so critical that the fate of the project and the management team lies on it. For this reason, financial audit is a major and sensitive event for the management team and sometimes a nightmare too. However, a project management team that understands the essence of the presence and modus operandi of Financial Auditors on its project and is well grounded on the management of the project will rather not be scared of the auditors but look forward to them, knowing that the end will add value to both the project and the team. In this light, this Chapter intends to position the project manager and his team to understand the purpose of financial audit; have an in roll into the process the audit may follow; appreciate the determinants and nature of auditor's opinion; and make preparations that guarantee auditor's affirmation of both the project and the management team. Forthwith, the financial audit referred to is external audit.

PURPOSE OF FINANCIAL AUDIT

It is usual that periodically, the financiers and other stakeholders in the project will like to know the state of the project – strengths, weaknesses, opportunities and threats emanating from financial issues in particular and the administration in general. Towards satisfying the project stakeholders' right to know, it is required that the project management team at the end of each period, usually one year, prepares and presents to the relevant stakeholders a financial document upon which they will base their assertion of the state of the project. This financial document is called Financial Statement. The financial statement provides an in-depth information on the project's financial position which also is dependent on the financial management of the project in particular and administrative management in general.

As the stakeholders are unlikely to trust the financial statement as presented by the project management team who ought not to be a judge in their own case, an independent External Auditor is engaged to consider the financial statement and ascertain the trueness of the document or otherwise in order to give the stakeholders confidence in their view regarding the project. This consideration by the external auditor constitutes the financial audit of the project. Financial auditing is primarily the act of expressing opinion on the financial statement prepared by the project as regards to its reliability, any omission or misstatement of accounting information due to whatsoever reasons. The auditor's process of determining these three conditions of the financial statements broadens the purpose of financial audit as such to include assessment of whether:

i. assets of the project are being properly safeguarded or not;
ii. transactions of the project are being recorded timely and as appropriate or not;
iii. accounts of the project are being maintained in conformity with accepted accounting principles necessary for the preparation of financial statement or not.

As a means of successfully carrying out these assessments is the evaluation of internal control that gives an indication of the manner of the handling of assets, transactions and accounts under the project. In this regard, financial audit purpose can be extended to include the evaluation of internal controls. Internal controls here are more of accounting controls which directly affect the figures indicated in the financial statement than administrative that may have indirect effect. The process of evaluating the internal control may by itself reveal existing or potential fraud and so, by implication, financial audit may have among its purposes the detection of frauds in the project.

In the case of projects financed by development agencies where the financiers will require the external auditor to pay attention to some specific things or acts, then these also would be part of the purposes of carrying out financial audit. Some of these acts may relate to finding out if:

i. all funds from the financier are being used exclusively for the purpose of the project and in accordance with the financing agreement conditions;
ii. all goods and services employed in the projects are being procured in accordance with financing agreement conditions;
iii. where a special account has been opened for the project, the operation is in accordance with the financing agreement conditions;
iv. fixed assets register is being maintained with verifiable ownership by the beneficiaries of the project in accordance with the financing agreement conditions.

In examining the above issues, therefore, as expected by the development agencies, the financial audit will not only require that the auditor expresses his opinion on the financial statements but also on the statements of expenditures and the project's special account.

FINANCIAL STATEMENTS

As the core subject of the financial audit is the review and evaluation of the project's Financial Statement, it is in the interest of the project manager and his team that they have ab-initio a proper understanding of the Financial Statements in terms of the constituents, purposes and interpretations.

Generally, according to International Financial Reporting Standards (IFRS), complete set of financial statements include:

i. Statement of Financial Position (Balance Sheet);
ii. Statement of Comprehensive Income (Income Statement);
iii. Shareholder's Funds;
iv. Cash Flow Statement; and
v. Explanatory Notes and Policies.

In more specific terms, for the development agencies' funded projects, as a requirement, the financial statements will include:

i. Balance Sheet;
ii. Statement of Income and Expenditures;
iii. Statement of Accumulated Fund;
iv. Statement of Expenditures;
v. Statement of Cash Flows;
vi. Statement of Special Account;
vii. Withdrawal-Disbursement Reconciliation; and
viii. List of Material Assets.

Balance Sheet

This is the most critical of the Financial Statements as it at a glance reveals the financial position of the project. It basically shows the assets, liabilities and accumulated fund. Because of the necessary interpretation of the balance sheet to assert the financial position of the project, these three items are further classified into, current assets, non-current (or fixed) assets, current liabilities and non-current liabilities. These classifications based IFRS definitions are understood as follows:

- **Assets:** resources of an entity resulting from past events and is such that has potential to yield future benefits to the entity;
- **Current Assets:** things the entity owns which the form can be changed within 12 months. Examples include cash, inventory, debtors, prepayments, etc.;
- **Non-current Assets:** things the entity owns which are fixed in nature, the form cannot easily change, and are part of the entity's infrastructure. Examples include property, equipment, furniture and fixtures, construction work-in-process, natural resources, goodwill, patents, etc. and development and research cost;
- **Liabilities:** present obligations of an entity due to past events and are such that the settlement will cause an outflow of the entity's economic resources;
- **Current Liabilities:** debts that are owed by the entity and should be repaid within 12 months. Examples include purchases from suppliers on credit (creditors), payments due but not yet paid (payables) e.g. wages, interest, taxes, etc.;
- Non-current Liabilities: debts that are owed by the entity and are repayable after 12 months. Example is long-term loans.

With the values of these components of the balance sheet known, a quick analysis can be carried out and deductions made on the financial position of the project. Some analysis typical of a development agencies' funded project may be in respect of net assets and liquidity ratios given as follows:

Net Assets	=	Total Assets – Total Liabilities
Working Capital	=	(Current Assets)/ (Current Liabilities) (%)
Acid Test	=	(Current Assets – Inventory)/ (Current Liabilities) (%)

A working capital ratio that is too high suggests that the assets are not being utilized effectively. On the other hand, an acid test of less than 100% indicates that the project may experience difficulties in paying its debt as at when due. Finally, a project is poised to higher danger as the net assets tend to zero. In addition to the analysis, a benchmark and/or yearly comparison of the values in the balance sheet can be made to determine if there is improvement in the financial position of the project in a given year, and if so or otherwise, by what percentage change from the previous years.

With this clear understanding of the purpose the balance sheet serves, the project manager and his team ought to be concerned about the values and therefore from the beginning of the project work towards commendable figures.

Statement of Income and Expenditures

This constitutes of receipts of funds into the project and expenditures made in respect of the project. If the receipts are from various sources such as the development agencies' funds and counterpart funds, each has to be separately indicated in the statement as such to make clear to the relevant stakeholders their respective cumulative contributions to the project.

The expenditures shown in the statement are categorized into heads according to the main activities or cost centers of the project. The details may be provided in the notes to the financial statements as appropriate.

The excess of receipt over expenditure will represent the cash and bank balances available to the project as at the date of the financial audit. If otherwise, it will raise suspicion.

Statement of Accumulated Fund

Accumulated Fund gives an indication of the residual interest by the financiers in the assets of the project after all the liabilities have been deducted. If the project was to be a business, the accumulated fund will be same as the shareholder's fund which is the equity contribution plus the cumulative retained profits over the years. Increasing size and positive percentage change of the accumulated fund compared with the previous years will signify improving turnover of the project.

Statement of Expenditures

In projects where the development agency permits disbursement methods such as Reimbursement and Special Account methods, the application for withdrawal is usually supported with Statement of Expenditures. Reimbursement method entails the reimbursement by the development agency of the expenses incurred and already paid for by the project. Special Account method involves the replenishment of the advance made by the development agency of which a part has been utilized by the project.

In supporting the request for disbursement using these methods, the statement of expenditures summarizes eligible expenditures incurred during a prior period to the request submission date. It is required that the project retain the respective statement of expenditure as submitted for each withdrawal application. At the time of financial audit, the auditor will check and express his opinion on the statements of expenditures with respect to the content's consistency with (1) date of incurring the expenses vis-à-vis the accompanying application (2) eligibility of the expenditure in terms of project activities and fund sources; and (3) terms and conditions of the legal financing agreement.

As negative outcome of any of the three can be highly injurious to the project and the management team, care need be taken to ensure the trueness and correctness of the statement of expenditures at all times.

Statement of Cash Flows

This shows the cash movement in the project for the period under audit. The inflows and outflows are shown in the statement. The net cash flows (inflows – outflows) represent the cash and cash equivalents at the project and bank. This ought not be neither too high nor low. While a high net cash flows may indicate that some activities are being delayed, low net cash flows may pose a challenge in meeting the project's immediate obligations.

Statement of Special Account

The Special Account as the name implies is exclusively for the project – to receive funds (reimbursement or replenishment) from the development agency and to carry out project related transactions. The only other inflow allowed into this account is the interest that the balances in the account may earn.

Matters that are critical to operating this account are the eligibility and correctness of financial transactions using the account, authority of the operators, and adherence to the terms and conditions of the legal agreement. As in the case of statement of expenditure, the auditor will check and express his opinion on these matters including the balance in the account at the end of the period hence it is imperative that care is taken by the project team in running the account.

Withdrawal-Disbursement Reconciliation

With the payment advice received from the development agency regarding disbursements and the records of receipts of funds by the projects, both are reconciled as appropriate. To avoid discrepancy in the future that may be difficult to reconcile, the project should keep proper withdrawal schedule and regularly update same accordingly.

List of Material Assets

This consists of tangible and non-current assets procured with the project funds. As the auditor may carry out physical verification of the assets of the project, it is important that the project maintains assets register that will reflect the purchase information, identification number, location and condition of the assets.

INTERNAL CONTROL

In addition to considering the financial statements of the project, the auditor will also directly express his opinion on the internal control of the project or indirectly use the outcome of his evaluation of the internal control to express his opinion on the financial statements. This, therefore, makes internal control a fundamental issue in the project that the project manager and his team need pay attention to. To do that, the concept and objectives of internal control must be well understood by the team.

Definitions and Scope of Internal Control

Internal control is a whole system established in order to provide reasonable assurance of effective and efficient operation; internal financial control; and compliance with laws and regulations (**Collier, 2009, p. 23**). It is a process put in place in the project based on policies and procedures - both internal and adopted, to ensure that the objectives of the project are achieved effectively and efficiently and that the financial statements produced in respect of the project are reliable and consistent with generally accepted accounting principles. Usually, this process is given effect by the governance, management and other personnel of the project and/or project host entity.

According to SAS No. 55, the internal control structure is made up of the control environment, the accounting system, and control procedures prevalent at the project. Control environment relates to the consciousness of the management towards internal control as observed in their attitude and style in dealing with the project's organizational structure;

governance; methods of assigning authority and responsibility; management control method; internal audit functions; personnel policies and practices; and external influences **(Wallace, 2005).** The accounting system entails methods of maintaining accountability for the project transactions – identification, classification, records and reporting of the project's assets and liabilities. Control procedures involve policies and procedures established or adopted to guarantee that the objectives of the project are achieved.

In terms of scope, **Wallace, 2005** reviewing the different definitions of internal control concludes that internal control in totality comprises:

i. the plan of organization;
ii. methods and procedures adopted within a business to ensure that goals and objectives are met;
iii. encouragement of adherence to prescribed managerial policies;
iv. means of ensuring that there is compliance with laws and regulations;
v. methods and measures to safeguard assets against waste, loss, and misuse;
vi. methods of promoting operational efficiency;
vii. means of gaining assurance that data obtained, maintained, and utilized by management are complete, accurate, and reliable; and
viii. means of gaining assurance that the adequacy of such data is also adequate in facilitating both the preparation of financial statements and the maintenance of accountability for assets and responsibility for liabilities.

Objectives of Internal Control

The primary objective of internal control is to provide reasonable assurance that in the course of the project:

i. assets are safeguarded;
ii. unauthorized use or disposition of the assets is prevented;
iii. unauthorized and/or bogus transactions are prevented;
iv. loss of information is avoided;
v. accounting of transactions is such that makes the resulting financial statements reliable; and
vi. ill motivated threats to best practices are detected and controlled;

This objective is in line with the view of Generally Accepted Governmental Auditing Standards (GAGAS). In order words, the whole essence of internal control or control system is to guarantee the integrity of financial accounting prepared based on it and most importantly to restrain threats to authorized policies and procedures, and best practices. Best practices are a set of guidelines, ethics or ideas that the application constitutes professional procedures acceptable as most efficient or prudent course of action that guarantee best results. Internal control is a reflection of the actions of the governance, management and personnel of the project aimed at the realization of the project's goals without compromising position, professionalism, competency, and integrity.

AUDITOR'S OPINION

The end result of the external audit of the project is having the external auditor express his opinion on both the financial statements and internal control prevalent at the project.

Therefore, the project manager or project management team expecting commendable outcome of the audit must be interested in the manner and the process leading to conclusive opinions of the auditor. In order words how and on what basis the auditor forms his opinion must be a concern to the project manager and his team, and therefore may as well be understood by them. This also requires that the basic areas of interest that the auditor is likely to focus to derive his opinion are accurately envisaged.

Audit Process

The audit process employed by the auditor is always geared towards enabling him express his opinion on the financial statements and the internal control of the project. The audit process can be grouped into three stages, namely, preliminary, active, and conclusion stages. All of these stages support the typical opinion process shown overleaf.

Figure 1: The Auditor's Opinion Process (Turn at 90°)

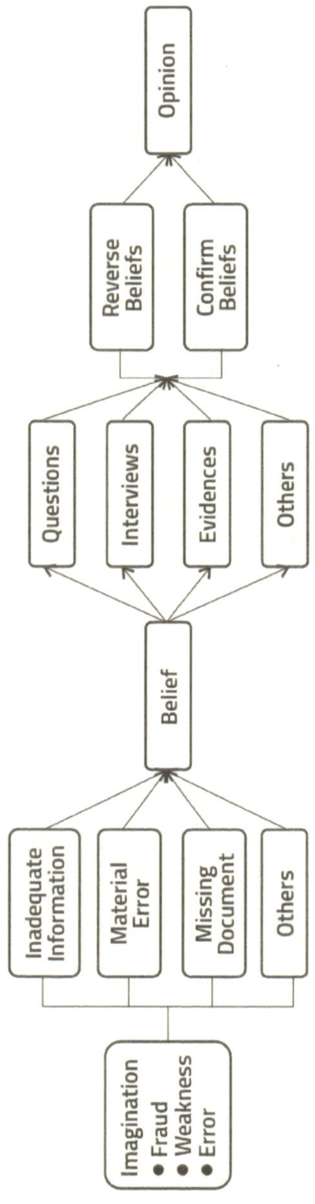

Preliminary Stage

As part of the preliminary stage of the audit, the first thing the auditor will do upon arrival at the project is to request for the project documents in order to acquaint himself with in-depth information regarding the project. Some of the information will include purpose, objectives and missions of the project; ownership and stakeholders; funding; completion date; etc. This information particularly in the case of development agencies' funded projects can be obtained from the following documents which are expected to be handy at the project:

- Strategic Plan;
- Financing Agreement;
- Project Appraisal Document;
- Project Implementation Manual;
- Rules and Procedures for Procurement;
- Disbursement Guidelines;
- Aide Memoires;
- Policies, procedures and records developed in the project over time; and
- Previous years audit reports and management letters.

Another aspect of the preliminary stage is the auditor's confirmation or otherwise of the auditability of the project. A project is auditable when it is established that for those transactions that affect financial operation of the project, there is proper filling and retention of the associated document as to enable audit. To ascertain this, the auditor checks if there is documentation for both routine and nonroutine transactions, the documents are prenumbered or coded, have proper authentication, maintained for sufficient period and filled in a reasonable order.

In the last part of this stage, the auditor will review the designed internal control in place. Based on this assessment, he will determine the adequacy of the internal control and the level of risk it poses to the achievement of project's objectives as expected. This preliminary assessment of the control risk is premised on the auditor's belief that even when there is compliance to already poorly designed internal control, its objective cannot be fully realized. An adjudged higher control risk will make extensive substantive testing of the project's transactions inevitable at the active stage of the audit.

Active Stage

The active stage of the audit is where the detection of material errors; fraud and corruption; and/or weaknesses of the internal control is preeminent. The auditor's mode at this point and as always is to exercise professional skepticism born out of the presumption that something may be wrong with the project – error in the accounts, weakness in the control or fraud. This fact about the auditor's disposition is one the project manager and his team need not be unmindful of. In pursuit of the purpose of the audit, the auditor may structure the project in terms of cost centers; cycles of operation, or subject matters, and examine the transactions respectively therein. The transactions may relate to purchases, sale of assets, procurement of contract, receipts and withdrawal of funds, contracts, foreign currency exchange, project activities, etc.

The auditor may gather his information necessary for the examination of the transactions through:

• Inquiry;

- Observation;
- Inspection; and
- Testing.

Of these channels, the most preferable to the auditor is testing as it provides him with the strongest evidence with respect to the validity of information; compliance with extant rules, policies and procedures; and correctness of numbers. On each transaction, he will check the critical information flow as per the conditions of authorization, the execution, the recording, and resulting assets (**Wallace, 2005**). While the conditions of authorization will include that the person giving the authorization has the capacity to do so; the execution of the transaction is expected to be within the terms of the authorization; and the recording, that the transaction is recorded at its amount; in the period in which it occurred; and under appropriate classification.

It is not unlikely that the auditor may narrow the examination of the transactions down to specific or chosen transactions of interest to him. Therefore, since the outcome of these few tests may be used to generalize on the weakness or otherwise of the internal control, every transaction should matter to the project management team.

Conclusion Stage

The conclusion stage of the audit process consists of the report on financial statements and issuance of management letter.

- *Report on Financial Statements*

This is a report that is independently produced by the auditors at the end of the audit exercise. Usually, it is not a cumbersome document; instead, it is brief and concise. The report which the primary purpose is to express an opinion on the project's financial statements is normally addressed to the apex authority in the governance of the project. For most projects funded by the development agencies, the apex authority is the steering committee. In this report, the auditor having expressed his opinion states the basis of his opinion. Expectedly, the basis of the opinion ought to be consistent with accepted standards such as International Standards on Auditing (ISA), accepted accounting policies, and the development agency's guidelines. Furthermore, the report indicates what had been the responsibilities of both the project management team and the auditor in the process of the audit. On the part of the project management team, it is the preparation and fair presentation of the financial statements. For the auditor, it is the audit of the financial statements and expression of an opinion on same accordingly. Finally, the report is accompanied with the audited financial statements of the project for use by the authorities, financiers, and other stakeholders.

- *Management Letter*

The management letter is a means by which the auditor:

- conveys his observations on the situation of the internal control as to the weaknesses; and effects of the weaknesses on the accounting system cum financial statements, safeguard of assets, and efficiency of operations;
- makes suggestions for changes to ameliorate the weaknesses and avoid the consequences; and
- reports on the inactions of the project management team

on the previous years' reported weaknesses that have remained prevalent.

The letter reflects the professional judgement of the auditors on the project. Though called a management letter, it is addressed to a replica of audit committee of board of directors for organizations, and for projects, the highest governing authority such as the steering committee in the case of most development agencies funded projects. In this letter, the auditor itemizes his observed concerns in the internal control and operations of the project indicating the subject areas or locations denominated in terms of cost centers or cycles of operation wherein the observed weaknesses exist. Some auditors may mention the respective office(s) or officer(s) directly responsible for weaknesses in question. The auditor based on his judgement classifies the observed weaknesses into material or immaterial and outlines the consequences or potential risks each portends to the accounting system, assets safety and efficient operations of the project. To curb these consequences or risks, the auditor also in this letter proffer solutions/suggestions that will consequently ensure that the objectives of the project is achieved. The suggestions are supposed to be constructive and give clear actions that will have the weakness or deficiencies corrected.

The management letter as produced is not conclusive at first instance since the auditor may offer the project management team the opportunity to provide written response to the issues raised. The project manager and his team should not be surprised that the letter will not blow up or promote the strong and positive performance of the team but may tend to be bias towards the project management deficiencies. It is all for the good and advancement of the project, and to also show that the auditor has done some detailed work.

When this draft is received, the project management team should not only be pliable, have open mind, and resolve to utilize the suggestions but also cease the opportunity to express its reservations on both the matter raised and the feasibility of the suggestions made by the auditor. They can also indicate their plan towards making good the unwanted conditions and eliminating the potential risks. Because of how important this letter and the response therein are, the process of providing the response should be taken very seriously by the project management team. All persons, particularly those whose line of duties have been questioned in the letter should be involved and under the coordination of project manager, a coherent response is supplied for inclusion in the final management letter.

It is not always that the project management team has the opportunity to make their views known in the management letter. Sometimes, the auditor may be reluctant to give this privilege to the project manager and his team in view of the following reasons:

- Want of cooperation from the project management team during the audit;
- Unhealthy control environment;
- Possible attempts by the project manager to justify his inactions;
- Possible undue persuasion by the project manager for the auditor to expunge some aspects of the letter.

Auditor's Key Areas of Interest

The key areas of interest of the auditor will depend on the terms of reference he has received for the audit. However, generally, based on standards, targeting to evaluate the operating effectiveness and efficiency of the project, the reliability of the financial statements, and compliance with laws, regulations and guidelines, the auditor will likely focus on some key areas during the audit. According to the COSO framework with internal control as the underlying subject of evaluation, the focus of an auditor usually will cover the following matter:

- Control Environment;
- Risk Assessment;
- Control Activities;
- Information and Communications;
- Monitoring;
- Safeguarding of Assets.

Without prejudice to the details of the COSO framework, simply put in line with the purpose of audit and in the way the project management team will understand, in the conduct of an audit, the auditor is actually looking for facts that will confirm or challenge the reliability on the financial statements prepared by the project. These facts may conclusively manifest in terms of auditor's observed:

i. Material weakness of control;
ii. Material error – intentional or unintentional; and
iii. Fraud.

The search for these facts to enable him form an opinion is what informs areas of interests of the auditor as he carries out the audit assignment. Typical key areas of interest that the auditors have always concentrated on include:

i. The Internal Control Design;
ii. Control Environment;
iii. Compliance;
iv. Duties and Responsibilities;
v. Transactions and Accounting;
vi. Fraud and Illegal Acts;
vii. Assets Management;
viii. Information and Communication;
ix. Internal Audit; and
x. Risks.

Internal Control Design

As a first step towards the identification of weakness of the internal control, the auditor will check the design and operations of the system as per its capability to either prevent or detect errors and fraud and generally have the control risk minimized to the extent that financial reporting of the project may be a representation of facts or misstatements. Reference to the design of the internal control will include recognition of the policies and procedures of the project, and laws and regulations. In the case of development agencies' funded projects, the design of the internal control will have as a component the provisions of the financial agreement, project appraisal document, procurement and financial management manuals, and other guidelines.

Control Environment

Usually, the auditor will observe the control environment which is reflected on the management's style, the organizational structure, the competence of the staff, the assignment of duties and responsibilities, the value placed on internal audit, ethics and integrity and the likes. The auditor's interaction with both the project staff and the management team will reveal the degree of existing control environment. Furthermore, checking the activities of the project's governance (e.g. steering committee) towards its specified role of providing necessary policy guidance and oversight on operations of the project will give an insight of the control environment.

Compliance

Having assessed the adequacy of the design of the internal control, the next thing the auditor will focus on is the extent of compliance being exhibited by project staff and management team. The best designed control will amount to nothingness if there is no compliance, just as perfect compliance to faulty internal control cannot achieve the purpose of internal control. The auditor will want to get an assurance that the planned internal control as per the policies and procedures are in use and being adhered to, thus, he will undertake tests of compliance (or tests of control). The extent, areas, or number of such tests will depend on the auditor's perception of the strength of both the different aspects of the designed internal control, and prevailing control environment.

Duties and Responsibilities

The auditor is likely to take a deeper look into how the duties of the staff and management are allotted. In this regard he will assess if there is sufficient segregation of duties in the operation and management of the project. Segregation of duties, according to **K.H Picket, 2005,** *is essentially not allowing one person to control an at-risk process.* Example of an at-risk process is such that involves requisition, payment, and stocking of an item. The auditor will check that one person does not start and finish any process within which there exist some risks that can be minimized by separation of duties. Additionally, the structure of the segregation should be such that allows distinct and independent responsibilities of authorization, verification and supervision.

Transactions and Accounting

How the accountability of the transactions in the project is maintained will be of great interest to the auditor. Subjects of checks as the auditor traces the documented transactions will include the identification, classification, records and reporting of resultant assets and liabilities. In this tracing, the information flow on the transaction with respect to authorization, execution, and transfer of value will as well be of importance. Although every transaction may matter to the auditor, depending on the area of the internal control design that he considers weak, he will carry out much of the tracing exercise of the transactions in that area. For obvious reasons, non-routine transactions of the project which the necessary procedures for execution may not be explicitly available will usually draw the attention of the auditor.

Fraud and Illegal Acts

Without mincing words, one of the things the auditor is looking out for is fraud or intention to commit fraud. Even though the auditor may question and receive answers from the project management team, he will choose to be skeptical of the responses as the target is to discover any inconsistencies between the facts evidenced and the explanations provided. From experience, the auditor becomes red alert when he observes:

- *Inadequate management oversight;*
- *Inadequate records;*
- *Incomplete duties;*
- *Insufficient or omitted authorizations and approvals;*
- *Poor or nonexistent physical safeguards.* (WALLACE, 2005)

What the auditor will be very much concerned with is where the system according to his judgement constitutes and creates incentives to perpetrate fraud or justify same. Under such condition, the simplest information not made available to the auditor at his request will further call for deeper attention. Generally, there are some threats in the project that will make the auditor more suspicious of fraud. These include:

- Rumors of fraud;
- Unexpected resignation of key staff;
- Disappropraite and unusual transaction;
- Abnormal payment or favour to staff;
- Avoidance of auditor's questions;
- Secrecy and excessive protection of workspace;
- Overvaluation of assets, improper revenue recognition;
- Misleading disclosures;

- Unrecorded transactions or event.

Regarding illegal acts, the auditor is likely to report the illegal acts as it portends adverse monetary implications that include fines, penalties and damages to the project. All of these will affect the financial statement now or in the future. The most dangerous aspect of discovering illegal act or fraud even when it is immaterial is that the auditor will no longer believe the staff or management's presentations in the different matters of the project and obviously will adjudge the control risk in the system very high.

Assets Management

The manner in which the physical assets of the project are procured, secured and disposed would be of great interest to the auditor. To confirm the adequacy and effectiveness of the assets' management, he will consider the existence and completeness of fixed assets register in terms of basic information such as description, procurement price and date, location, physical condition and residual value. Upon physical inspection, the auditor will like to see that the assets are tagged and coded and conform to the information provided in the assets register. Also, the concern of the auditor in the assets' management will be the way assets are disposed – whether due process is followed or not.

Information and Communication

The project management's recognition of essential information and its process, time and recording of the communication are issues the auditor will not ignore. The auditor will be interested on how open reasonable sources of information (internal and external) has been maintained and how the communications have been effected as not to mar strategic decisions for the progress and achievement of the project objectives. For instance, he may consider how the work plan, budget, approvals including no-objections are circulated to enable staff undertake their responsibilities responsibly, effectively and timely.

Internal Audit

The auditor will in the audit process pay strong attention to how the internal auditor has been fulfilling his traditional roles in the project as required. Some of the issues the auditor will evaluate vis-à-vis the internal auditor's pursuit of 'value for money' for the project's operations will include:

- Roles of the internal auditor on the project – definitions and scope;
- Relative autonomy and independence of the internal auditor;
- Exclusivity of the activities of the internal auditor with the project's normal accounting functions;
- Qualification and capacity of the internal auditor;
- Reporting of the internal auditor to the top management – regularity, circulation, and reviews of findings and recommendations with the appropriate authorities; and
- Effectiveness of the follow-up actions of the internal auditor.

Risks

The subject of risks in the project will also be considered by the auditor. According to **Kerzner, 2017**, risk is "a measure of the probability and consequence of not achieving a defined project goal". Risk as per the entire project is a wide subject that the auditor may not fully cover in the financial audit but obviously those that are related to financial management will matter much to him. For instance, he will have interest on the project team's handling of financial risk management instruments such as Advance Payment Guarantee, Performance Security, Letter of Credit, etc.

Expression of Auditor's Opinion

According to the key areas of interest discussed above, the auditor will express his opinion in the report on financial statements and management letter due for submission at the end of the audit. The opinion of the auditor is very critical and therefore cannot be regarded as inconsequential by the project management team. Having professional responsibility, the auditor will not fail to report and express his opinion on all matters bothering on financial management, internal control and governance that currently or have the potentials to contribute to faulty financial statements and/or inefficient operation that may affect the achievement of the project's objectives.

The language of the auditor in expressing his opinion is simple and concise particularly on the issue of financial statements. For the financial statements, most times after the rigorous exercise of audit, the opinion is expressed as an affirmation or otherwise of this highly valued question – does the financial statements as presented give, in all material respects, a true and fair view of the financial position of the project and other financial information provided for the period covered by the audit?. This is apparently all that are required of the auditor to state concerning the financial statements. On the other aspects of the audit, particularly the internal control, the manner of the auditor's opinion is by qualification of the control in terms of its strength to ensure operational efficiency and avoid or detect fraud, and material errors in the financial statements. On the basis of the control risks test conducted, the auditor, for the results on the negative side will assert either, internal control deficiency, or non-material weakness or material weakness in his opinion with respect to certain or whole of the procedures of the internal control. The PCAOB defines control deficiency and material weakness conditions respectively as those wherein:

> *"the design or operation of a control does not allow management or employees, in the normal course of performing their assigned functions, to prevent or detect misstatements on a timely basis"*

> *"a significant deficiency, or combination of significant deficiencies, that results in more than a remote likelihood that a material misstatement of the annual or interim financial statements will not be prevented or detected"*

Further distinctive conditions attracting auditor's opinion as non-material weakness or material weakness of the observed internal control are shown in *Table 1* below. The significance of the declaration of material internal control weakness is that the condition, if not already, has the potential to in the future adversely affect the financial statements, safeguard of the assets and efficient operations of the project.

Table 1: Conditions and Categorization of Internal Control Weakness

S/N	Observed Internal Control Conditions	Non-Material Weakness	Material Weakness
1	A necessary procedure is not in place.		
2	There exists non-compliance with a certain procedure.		
3	The certain procedure is such that the non-compliance will result to substantial misstatement and/or fraud.		
4	There exists non-compliance with a significant number of procedures.		
5	There exists audit difference, but it is due to adoption of different accounting principles.		
6	There exists audit difference, but it is not traceable to the difference in accounting principles and could not have been detected by the procedures in place.		

In the cases of fraud and illegal acts observed during the audit, the auditor is always careful with the language he uses to report them. It all depend on whether it is just a suspicion in which case the matter has not been verified, then the auditor has to enshrine his statement with a disclaimer or the act has or can be determined to have occurred, the auditor is assertive and if possible, indicates the impact.

In addition to the mere judgmental expression of his opinion, the auditor may advance to analytical based opinion. This involves for instance, referring to a number of fundamentals of the project and internally (or externally for typical projects) making comparison of two point in times; and using a single benchmark to form opinions in the current audit.

Conclusively, as an expression of his opinion in the audit report, the auditor for each of the observed weaknesses follows a particular pattern in his reporting. He first cites properly the observed weakness to convey the real issues, and secondly, indicates explicitly the implication and consequences of that weakness both now and in the future if it persists, and thirdly provides suggestions to ameliorate or eliminate the weakness and the predicted consequences, and finally, highlights the advantages of his recommendations if implemented.

MEETING THE AUDITOR'S EXPECTATIONS DELIBERATELY

Armed with forgoing knowledge of the purpose of audit, process of audit, and nature of the auditor's opinion, it is of necessity that the project management team deliberately prepares and works to satisfy the auditor. Some of the measures that the team may take as such to have confidence that the project will have the commendation of the auditor should touch on the design of the internal control, staff buy-in and diligence in the operation of the internal control, management of transactions, prevention of fraud, promotion of ethical behavior and integrity, and conduct of self-audit.

Design of the Internal Control

Fundamentally, internal control in the context of adding value to the project is the application of procedures that guarantee the integrity of financial accounting prepared based on the said procedures, and are consistent with best practices wherein mechanism for control and detection of ethical abnormalities are operational in the project. In this regard, the design of these procedures is critical if the desired internal control purpose must be accomplished. The design must result to procedures that not only promote accountability, transparency and protection of assets, but serve as a way of doing things right, and towards achieving the project's objectives, and stopping problems escalating out of control. While setting boundaries, the design must aim at procedures that are effective and efficient in operation and cost. To achieve such design, five basic steps are necessary for the project management team to take:

- Have a clear definition and understanding of the project objectives in terms of performance, time and cost;
- Based on the understanding of the project, establish the underlying processes required to achieve the objectives and break them into tasks that further are grouped into operational framework, e.g. departments, sales, purchases, contract procurements, phases, etc.;

- Identify the risks that are associated with each of the cycles of the operational framework. Risks here are threats to best practices towards projects' performance, time and cost; irregularities that may occur such as unauthorized and exaggerated transactions, mishandling of information and assets, and inaccurate records;
- Develop controls around the identified risks in each of the cycle of the operational framework as such to manage, mitigate or avoid the occurrence of the threat; and
- Conduct cost-benefit analysis of the developed controls iteratively and finally adopt the considered appropriate controls.

When designing internal control for the project, it is important to ensure that the control is consistent with basic standards that allow for:

- Segregation of duties – disintegration of at-risk process (e.g. movement of cash from start to finish)
- Authorization – the act of one person authorizing another to discharge his duties
- Security – unauthorized person never gets access to both material and information not relevant to him or his operations; 'preventative control'.
- Identification Codes – 'detective control'
- Verification – checks: inventory, assets, etc.
- Supervisory review – review other people's work.

Put in another way, **Wallace, 2005** has recommended that in designing internal control an attempt should be made to answer the following questions in order to have the outcome meet the expectations of the auditor:

- *Are control and operating responsibilities appropriately segregated?*
- *Are all transactions being recorded in the accounting system?*
- *Has management created an environment for effective control?*
- *Have checks and balances been established?*
- *Has operating efficiency been appropriately considered?*

One key consideration requiring emphasis in the internal control design is the segregation of job responsibilities. The principle is that for a particular transaction, different people should exclusively undertake the authorization of the initiation, the custody of the resulting assets and the record keeping of the accounts. The idea is that fraud and misappropriation are easily perpetuated where one person undertakes two or all of these functions than when each is handled independently by a person. In this case, the possibility of colluding to commit crime is minimized. The same principle needs to be adopted even when the system is computerized. Although the IT administration by its position and activities may have access to the server leading to all operations, access to different level of the transaction process must be limited by functions of the employees. In order words, approval at different levels of the system must be done by different people.

As both the finance and keeping of assets are high risk areas in terms of safeguarding the project's assets, attention must be paid to them and high-level internal control design covering fund receipts, expenditures, administrative costs, documentation in support of transactions, etc. established.

On the other hand, without prejudice to the foregoing,

the design of internal control should not stifle but facilitates operating efficiency of the project. Creative thinking must be involved instead of being endangered. Within the reasonable bounds, internal control should promote creativity and innovation which are also essential for achieving project's objectives. Excess of anything may not be good. Where internal control gets to the extreme, bureaucracy is the result. And this may inhibit the smooth operations and not allow structured innovation desirable for the project performance.

Finally, the design of the internal control of the project even if in operation cannot be said to be complete if it is not properly documented. The project management team has to prove to the auditor that internal control exists by first showing him the approved procedures (set of instructions that describes a task or process) in form of policies, operational manuals (technical, financial and administrative), and guidelines – internally produced or exogenously adopted. Secondly, the auditor will be impressed to see that these documents are also living – in order words, the operations are being assessed from time to time and the design suitably amended periodically. These will indicate a reasonably healthy and active control environment.

Staff buy-in and Diligence in the Operation of the Internal Control

From the perspective of effective internal control, the operation must be anchored on ownership, competence, and compliance, all of which are driven by the attitude, knowledge and skill of the staff of the project. The staffs have a major role to play in the operation of the internal control and this must start from the point of ownership of the system. And to own, it is expedient that the staff participate in the design of the internal control ab-nitio. It will interest the auditor to know that the staff were actually involved in the design and seen by their conduct to have a buy-in in the prevalent internal control.

Associated with the staff participation in the design of the internal control is their understanding of the complete system. The ground for internal control is the operation of systems that work to form a single system. The individual staff role is to make the sub-systems work. Therefore, for efficient and effective system of internal control to be realized, each of the staff must have a global perception of the system and irrespective of independence of each sub-system consider the interdependencies and its contributions towards the overall good of the system. This is why a full understanding of the procedures and relevance of the processes is required, and sure will enhance capacity of the staff and project management team and make control easier.

Another element necessary for the operation of internal control the auditor will appreciate in the project is the competence of the staff. It will be interesting to observe the great knowledge, expertise and positive common sense the staff deployed in getting things done right towards achieving the project's objectives. In this sense, how qualified and skillful the staffs are, exhibiting reasonable responsibility and intellectual freedom will matter to the auditor. Therefore, among the measures to satisfy the auditor are to have in the staff body well qualified personnel and also, relate staff performance assessment to attitude towards the set internal control. As part of achieving these, training of the staff on the applicable procedures in the project is key. The focus of such training should include the role of the staff in the integration of the sub-systems to a whole system where fragmentation is thinned out and the overall project objectives are achieved. It is better to train the staff well on the internal control than to have compliance team police the system.

Talking about compliance, when internal control is internalized by the staff, compliance becomes a non-issue. These days, enforcement of compliance is no longer a preferred option as modern management will emphasize on coaching rather than driving staff to automated compliance. Coaching involves encouraging staff and developing them to assuming responsibility that is rational and imperative to the achievement of the organizational goals. Rather than being robotlike, a highly motivated staff goes beyond acting exclusively to protect his job but make concerted efforts following due process to contribute to the objectives of the project. Above all, in anticipation of the coming of the external auditor, the general philosophy of the staff as he performs his function should be 'you too, is an auditor'. This will build a sense of responsibility on the part of all to be conscious of ethical values required and necessary for good practices leading to the achievement of project's objectives.

Management of Transactions

The driving mindset on the management of transactions of the project should be founded on the fact that the tasks of the expected auditor include to, according to PCAOB *"determine the level of detail and degree of assurance that would satisfy prudent officials in the conduct of their own affairs that they have reasonable assurance that transactions are recorded as necessary to permit the preparation of financial statements in conformity with generally accepted accounting principles".* This places strong responsibility on the project management team to ensure that all transactions of the project are treated appropriately to guarantee the desired assurance.

Preliminary management of the transactions in anticipation of the auditor requires that a critical information flow on each transaction satisfy these three basic criteria relating to authorization, execution and recording:

- conditions of authorization must include that the person giving the authorization has the capacity to do so;
- the execution of the transaction must be within the terms of the authorization;
- the recording of the transaction must be such that the transaction is: 1) recorded in its amounts; (b) recorded in the period in which it occurred; and (3) classified as appropriate.

Pivotal to issue of transaction is the documentation even though authorization, avoidance of bogus transactions and safeguarding of the resulting assets are equally important. Documentation plays key role in the financial management of projects. Documentation entails the recording of the transactional activities structured along the operations of the project and the associated financial implications of the activities categorized according to the appropriate chart of accounts. For example, acquisition of capital, procurement of contracts, selling of goods or services, investments, disposal of assets, etc. The substance of true documentation both for internal control and audit purposes must consider two things, the filling system and document control.

Filling System

The filling of the document which may be paper or electronic must be done in a particular order (chronological, location, thresholds, etc.) for a transaction or related financial operations. The filling should be such that makes it easy to trail a transaction. The files themselves should be maintained for a reasonable period before being disposed.

Document Control

Document control begins with the nomenclature – system of naming documents, e.g. receive notes, instructions, local purchase order, project components, etc. To have effective document control, all the document particularly the printed forms must be prenumbered and periodically be checked to ensure that the sequence is intact. It is also important that where the document demands approval, and arithmetical or other checks, the personnel carrying out the function do initialize it. This does not exclude computerized process. On another note, to maintain document control, even the voided forms must be retained in the system as a missing number in the series may suggest intention to commit fraud.

Of note are non-routine transactions which usually draw the attention of the auditor. Serious attention must be paid in the documentation of such transaction to ensure that it is executed with best practice particularly where there are no written procedures for such transaction.

Prevention of Fraud

There are three factors that are known catalysts to fraud in projects and therefore require the focus of the project management team in an attempt to prevent fraud. These are situational pressure; opportunity to commit fraud; and lack of integrity. Whilst the former two can be reasonably controlled through the internal control in place, the later depends on the personality of the individuals that make up the management and staff of the project. Unfortunately, it has been observed that most of the frauds committed in projects even when the two promotional factors of pressure and opportunity are present are products of lack of integrity. Therefore, towards preventing fraud, one major step is to be mindful of the kind of people that are employed in the project. This is difficult but a little due diligence and some counseling on the dangers of severe sanctions may help.

Ultimately, internal control appears to be the strongest instrument that can be used to prevent frauds. If the internal control is effectively working and the internal audit functioning, the propensity to commit fraud will be minimized as the fraud signals are likely to be noticed and early steps taken to prevent it. Some of these signals include:

- Rumors of fraud;
- Unexpected resignation of key staff;
- Disappropraite and unusual transaction;
- Abnormal payment or favour to staff;
- Secrecy and excessive protection of workspace;
- Overvaluation of assets, improper revenue recognition;
- Misleading disclosures;

- Unrecorded transactions or event.

In addition to these signals, some conditions that the project team management needs also to check and avoid the existence in order to mitigate the rate of acceleration of fraud in projects include:

- Over familiarities of some personnel with the vendors
- Inadequate communication on the policies and procedures;
- Unseriousness in upholding the policies and procedures;
- Withholding of due sanctions to offending personnel;
- Disharmony in the management team;

It is in the interest of the team to make deliberate efforts towards countering the threats of frauds and ensure they do not occur. If frauds are adequately prevented in the project, the auditor will see nothing and will report nothing.

Promotion of Ethical Behavior and Integrity

Again, ethical and integrity disposition are rooted on the persons conviction, morals, and values. These are characteristics that are internally driven. The much that can be done by the management team is first to live by example and regularly communicate the essence of doing things in the most acceptable way void of conflicting interest, selfishness, greed and disregard for best practices.

The vision of the project must be made clear to include transparency, accountability and sustainability. The project management team and the staff whenever individually or collectively want to take any action as the project is being implemented must ask the question whether or not the action is:

- Characterized by conflict of interest;
- Legal;
- Right;
- Beneficial; or
- One that devalues one's reputation in the public eye if exposed.

As part of promoting ethics and integrity in the system, there must be known sanctions that are not only contained in the project's procedures and policies but indeed await whoever acts contrary to the above ethical questions. To help also in this regard, frequent related trainings should be conducted for the team and staff hoping that minds of will continually get positively renewed. How great it will be to have the financial audit of the project end with the auditor not having any reason to fault the actions of any.

Conduct of Self-Audit

The final measure that the project management team has to take to prepare and expect the commendation of the auditor is the conduct of self-audit prior to the arrival of the auditors.

It is usual that the project management team prepares the financial statement that would be audited by the auditor but much more than simply having the Statement, the wise thing to do is to have an in-dept and critical look at the state and readiness of the project for a favorable audit. The team should put itself in the position of an external auditor and follow the process a rational auditor will adopt and examine seriously the areas the auditor will likely take interest in. In this regard, self-audit will require an examination of the instant internal control and check on those areas which will include:

- The Internal Control Design;
- Control Environment;
- Compliance;
- Duties and Responsibilities;
- Transactions and Accounting;
- Fraud;
- Assets Management;
- Information and Communication;
- Internal Audit; and
- Risks.

The self-audit will reveal the financial management deficiencies in the project and offer the project management team the opportunity to make amends when it is not too late. Knowing that the auditor will surely come one day, it will make no sense waiting for the management team and the project to have their inadequacies exposed when they could have been corrected.

A positive outcome of external audit confers on project management team respect from all stakeholders and provides the confidence for the team to perform even much better. On the contrary, a qualified and negative audit not only attracts disrespect and probable sanctions against the management team but can bring the project to sudden and sad end.

CHAPTER THREE

PERFORMANCE AUDIT

PERFORMANCE AUDIT is one of the audits that a project is not likely to escape in its life-cycle. It may come up once or severally during the initiation, planning, execution or after completion of the project. This is why the project management team needs to have thorough knowledge of and indeed expect the conduct of performance audit on its project at any time.

Understanding Performance Audit

Performance audit is an independent assessment of the project to determine firstly the achievements of the defined project's objectives reflected by the inputs, outputs, results and impacts, and secondly the efficiency, economy and effectiveness of the operations in attaining the achievements.

Performance audit in its primary approach focuses on the employed inputs and realized outputs, results and impact, and not so much of the control system encapsulated in policies and procedures, and the compliances since successful achievements of project objectives is not likely to occur in the absence of healthy control system. The concentration is on the quantity, quality and cost of the concerned inputs, outputs, results and impact.

One should not mistake performance audit for financial audit or evaluation as they are not the same. While performance audit assesses the project achievements vis-à-vis economy, efficiency and effectiveness, financial audit assesses the legality and regularity of financial operations and reliability of the financial statements. Using the concept of accountability, **Nalewaik and Mills, 2014** gives a good illustration to distinguish the two. Referring to the use of money in the project, financial audit will require the assessment of the compliance with authorization procedures and recording of the transactions resulting from the use, while performance audit will check how appropriate, efficient and effective both the authority and the money have been utilized.

On the other hand, evaluation is closely related to performance audit. Both provide assessment of economy, efficiency and effectiveness but the contexts in which they take place differ. Further difference is that accountability test is more central in performance audit than in evaluation which sometimes has its results included as part of the information for performance audit.

Purpose and Relevance of Performance Audit

The purpose of performance audit is to upon independent assessment of the project's performance make recommendations such that the implementation will contribute to the improvement of the performance of the project in terms of the quantity, quality and cost of the inputs, outputs, results and impacts.

Performance audit provides an assurance or otherwise to the project stakeholders concerning the project's achievements and their sustainability; the economy, efficiency and effectiveness with which the project is being operated, and the chances of meeting the project's objectives. Beyond addressing the expectations of the stakeholders of the project, performance audit most importantly provides an opportunity for improvement. According to **European Court of Auditors' Performance Audit Manual**, some of the improvements might involve:

- financial savings;
- better working methods;
- avoidance of waste;
- more cost-efficient achievement of stated objectives.

Generally, as highlighted by **Nalewaik and Mills, 2014,** the relevance of performance audit includes:

- Facilitation of continuous improvement;
- Support to learning culture;
- Strengthening of accountability and controls;
- Enablement in transparency in report; and
- Contribution to good governance

Basis of Performance Audit

The basis of performance audit is in two parts, namely, nominal performance basis and real performance basis. Basis here relates to the classification, condition, value or subject that the assessment is referenced to.

Nominal Performance Basis

Nominal performance audit entails referencing the assessment only to the output, outcome and impact of the project. At this level of assessment, what is paramount is how much? –

of the outputs, the outcomes, and the impacts with reference to the expected. The expected is not indefinite and therefore need to be established. If these expected are not established at the initiation of the project, the onus lies on the project management team to do so at some point considered the base date knowing that the performance audit would later be based on them.

A typical project will have the expected outputs, outcomes, and impacts contained in the Result Measurement Framework (RMF) consistent with theory of change wherein project activities result to outputs, and outputs give rise to outcomes, and the outcomes create the impact. The performance indicators which are the proofs of realization of the outputs, outcomes and impact are also provided in the RMF. Furthermore, for clarity on what constitutes performance in the project, the performance indicators are well defined in the RMF. The unit of measure, baseline, and interim and final target measures of each performance indicator are also provided in the RMF. All of these forms the basis of the performance audit at the nominal level and therefore must be well understood and taken cognize of by the project management team.

Real Performance Basis

For real performance audit, the basis of the assessment beyond the nominal is extended to the economy, efficiency, and effectiveness observed by the project management team in the achievement or otherwise of the outputs, outcomes and impacts of the project. The assessment of the three Es' is predicated on the common question of if the right thing was done by the project management team at every point in time and process in a given circumstance towards optimal achievement of the project objectives.

Economy

Economy relates to getting input at the best price that can result to a given output. It borders on whether the best deal was obtained in executing an activity in the project. Where the cost of inputs is reduced for a given level (quantity and/or quality) of output, waste and overpayment are avoided. Another aspect of economy is the issue of alternative approach, processes and deployment of inputs that could have resulted to lower costs in achieving yet the project's objectives. Generally, economy looks at the project's elements and overall cost of resources employed relative to the quantity and quality of outputs obtained.

Efficiency

Efficiency relates to obtaining the best results (quantity and/or quality of outputs) with a given input. It is all about being productive and using resources well as such that an output increases without having to have the inputs increase. In order words, outputs are produced cost effectively and the input/output ratios are most optimal. Where this is the case, it is a proof that wastes are minimized and leakages avoided. Leakages is seen to occur when the quantum of resources employed do not lead to the desired and reasonable output. Both waste and leakages in projects may involve materials, labour, plants, overheads, moneys and most importantly, time.

Some of the project's implementation processes and tools that the handling is likely to bear on economy and efficiency separately or collectively and become subject of the auditor's examination include:

- Organizational Strategy
- Work Plan;
- Works Methodology;
- Activity Scheduling and Timing;
- Technical Specifications;
- Budget;
- Financing;
- Cash Flow Management;
- Procurement of goods, works and services;
- Contract Delivery
- Standard Costs and Benchmarks

Effectiveness

Effectiveness means getting the right results; It is all about achieving project's objectives whatever they are. Quantity and the quality of the quantities as desired of the project are key here. The assessment of effectiveness relates to the extent to which the outputs, outcomes and impacts culminating in the objectives of the project are met. Under effectiveness check, the achievements of the project's objectives incorporating a measure of the outputs, outcomes and impacts are assessed in terms of the internal operations (internal workings) or time, categorized into, immediate, intermediate and overall as may have been provided in the Monitoring and Evaluation Plan produced from the Result Measurement Framework of the project. The audit focusing on effectiveness is more or less the nominal performance audit as discussed earlier.

Performance Audit Process and Audit Evidence

Like other forms of audits that may be witnessed in a project, performance audit has a process which is important the project management team is acquainted with and shore up itself. Although unlike financial audit, there is not yet a common standard of the process, but the intent of the performance audit and the stakeholders' expectations of the audit will determine the scope and the process the auditor will employ in the audit. The common process as observed by **Nalewaik and Mills, 2017** include:

> *"Kick-off meeting, document requests, interviews and/or workshops, review of documentation, development of findings, meeting with the client to discuss findings and issues, and a formal report and presentation"*

According to the **European Court of Auditor's Performance Audit Manual, 2017** which details much of what at the moment may be considered best practice, the place to start in the performance audit process is to set the audit objectives, and define what constitutes audit evidence and how the findings will be derived and the conclusions made.

The project management team may not be aware what precisely are the objectives of the performance audit, but it should not be indifferent of the constituents of the audit evidences the auditor will collect to assert his findings and express his opinion on the project performance. The nature of these evidences may vary from physical, documentary, oral, to analytical. Physical evidences are those the auditor captures through inspection and observation, such as physical work-in-progress or outputs (assets), and events. Documentary evidences are obtained through the review of the project documents including agreements, reports, manuals, contracts, letters, policies and procedures and other document that may be contained in the project files. Constituting the oral evidences are the recorded (minutes, audio or video) interviews, focus groups, inquiries or panels. Finally, analytical evidences entail expertise deductions through appropriate analysis (ratio, variance, regression, trend, comparative, benchmarking, etc) of the data arising from the other three evidences.

It is important to note that the sources of these evidences are not exclusively the project. The auditor may refer to publications (laws, studies and research, expert opinions, etc.), as well as the beneficiaries of the project, the contractors and other interest groups to have new evidences or additional ones to collaborate the project's sourced evidences.

The Performance Auditor's Report and Opinion

For most development agencies' funded project, a typical performance audit report's structure will consist of four sections, namely:

- Executive Summary;
- Implementation Performance;
- Assessment Results; and
- Issues, Lessons and Follow-up Actions.

The executive summary gives a brief of the purpose and outcome of the performance audit. The second section of the report deals with the performance of the implementation activities. Here, the auditor discusses the rationale and the workability of the executing arrangement of the project as observed; the expected quality, time and cost of the project is compared with the actual giving details of the cause and effects of the observed procedures and actions of the management, contractors, suppliers and consultants. Most reported of these procedures and actions are those that relate to procurement, contract award, contract administration, inputs and outputs of the project. The financing of the project and management of the cash flow is also discussed here. Furthermore, governance of the project and compliance to the covenants of the financing agreement are also highlighted.

The third section of the report, assessment results, is where based on the findings of the auditor, his judgement of the implementation performance is expressed as the audit opinion. Usually, this judgement qualifying the performance according to the economy, efficiency and effectiveness, will rely on the measure of the findings against:

- *Legislation, regulations, professional standards;*
- *Standards, measures or results commitments of the project ab-nitio;*
- *Performance of comparable organisations, best practice, or standards developed by the auditor.* (**ECA Manual, 2017**)

With weights assigned by the auditor to economy, efficiency, and effectiveness as appropriate in line with the audit's defined objectives, the overall rating of the project performance is determined. For most performance audits, the final rating constituting the auditor's opinion is in terms of relative success as follows, highly successful, successful, partly successful, and unsuccessful.

The last section of the report highlights the earlier reported issues that have remained unresolved; the lessons that can be learnt by the wide range of stakeholders with regards to the performance; and the specific matters of the project that actions are required within a certain period going forward.

While the above gives an overview of what is expected of the structure of the reports of the performance audit from development agencies' projects perspective, **Nalewaik and Mills, 2017** have developed a more encompassing segmentation of the performance audit enabling concentration to eight modules without leaving any aspect of the project unattended to. The modules with their respective goals as per guiding the reviewer are as follows:

i.	Planning:	Matching objectives with long-term strategy;
ii.	Stakeholders:	Defining success;
iii.	Risk:	Optimizing opportunities;
iv.	Compliance:	Responding to internal and external requirements;
v.	Resources:	Focusing on economy and efficiency;
vi.	Management Controls:	Improving effectiveness;
vii.	Post-Project:	Customer satisfaction and future planning;
viii.	Special Issues:	Targeted review of specific concerns and risks.

(**Nalewaik and Mills, 2017**)

Positioning the Project for High Performance Rating

Equipped with this information on the purpose, process, areas of concentration and rating pattern of performance audit, the right question that the project management team need ask is 'what shall we do to have our project receive high rating from the performance auditors'. The answer is not farfetched. It is all about the project management team working assiduously to achieve the desired project objectives and being deliberate in its actions in anticipation, rightfully too, of the likely conduct of performance audit on the project in the future by an independent entity. To do this, there are some tools and elements of project management that the team will need to pay much attention to and focus on as best practices in these aspects of management are poised to contribute to the overall economy, efficiency and effectiveness of the project which are the subjects of the performance audit. These include:

- Organizational Strategy;
- Work Planning;
- Works Methodology;
- Activity Scheduling and Timing;
- Technical Specifications;
- Budgeting;
- Financing;
- Cash Flow Management;
- Procurement Management for goods, works and services;
- Contract Management;
- Standard Costing and Benchmarking;

In order for the management team to assert itself as qualifying for commendation from the auditors, the team must understand the essence of each of these aspects, tools, or element of project management, and anticipate specific interests of the auditors in these subjects, and show that the team is exercising best practices as regards to these areas. Therefore, following below is a discussion of each of these essential management activities presented as such to provide hands-on manual and check list for self-audit of the project management team towards meeting the auditor's expectations.

WORK PLAN

Work Plan is a fundamental document that reflects the vision for the performance of the project. Without a Work Plan, the passion normally created by vision will be absent and sure will lead to non or poor performance of the project. This is why Work Plan is a major document that the performance auditor will always be interested to observe the existence, creation and use as tool by the project management team for the enablement of the realization of the project objectives. With respect to the project, Work Plan provides answers to the questions of what, and what needs to be done, how each can be accomplished, who is to do each, where and when each has to be done and at what cost. With all of these resolved in advance, the document serves as a tool for coordinating the activities and helping the project management team to control each in terms of scope, quality, time of execution and cost. By its use also, progress cum performance of all aspects of the project is measured relative to the baseline and target.

Focus of the Performance Auditor

Considering the importance of the Work Plan, it is pertinent that the project management team know exactly what the interests of the performance auditor are regarding the Work

Plan. There are basically two aspects of the Work Plan that matter to the performance auditor as he carries on with the assessment. Firstly, is the quality of the Work Plan and secondly, the implementation of the Work Plan. There is a direct relationship between the quality of the Work Plan and performance of the project. A qualitative Work Plan is likely to result to a higher performance. So also is effective implementation of the Work Plan.

The quality of the Work Plan as it concerns the project relates to:

- Scope of the plan (the coverage);
- Structure and integration of the elemental plans;
- Simplicity, understandability and Relevance of the information contained in the plan;
- Reality of the bases of the plan;

A good Work Plan will be such that shows that all the activities necessary to have the project completed as required are identified; these activities have realistic duration allotted to them and are arranged in proper sequential order; appropriate persons or entities are marked for the execution; and sensible estimated costs are provided. Above all, the performance auditor's focus is to check the potentials of this document in satisfying the desired purpose of the Work Plan. In order words, can the Work Plan as initially produced or revised promote the followings enabling excellent performance of the project:

- Early completion of the project;
- Knowledge of project milestones;
- Uninterruption of activity and cash flows;

- Effective communication among the project management team including other stakeholders;
- Minimized confusion and misunderstanding;
- Accountability of persons in charge;
- Cost control;
- Monitoring and evaluation; and
- Risks mitigation.

Beyond the quality of the Work Plan is most importantly its implementation driven by the project management team as expected. This is another focus of the performance auditor. Measure of implementation of the good Work Plan will determine the measure of the success of the project. It will be of interest to the performance auditor to know how the 'start' time and 'end' time of various activities contained in the Work Plan are being respected. An aggregated late starts and late end of many activities will obviously result to delays and unlikely accomplishment of the interim or final project objectives. And where achieved, it may be at a higher cost compared with the expected. The observed high margin of disparity between the planned and actual will not only indicate to the performance auditor poor performance but constitute a threat to future accomplishment of either part or the entire project at the right time and cost.

Preparation of the Work Plan

In view of the expected focus of the performance auditor, the preparation of the Work Plan as such to make it qualify as a quality plan is critical for the project management team and therefore requires basic knowledge. The areas demanding attention include the participants in the planning, time of preparing the plan, information necessary for the planning, and the actual development of the plan.

Planning Participants

The first wrong step towards the preparation of a good Work Plan is for one person or a very few persons to sit down alone and produce a plan. A proper Work Plan starts with the involvement of members of the project management team and the consultation with other stakeholders in the project; all of whom have had the chance to acquaint themselves with the project requirements.

The preparation is a team work so much as the final document is expected to cover all aspects of the project including key activities, persons or entities responsible for the activities, and the delivery method, time and cost of the activities. Given the opportunity, all of these would be identified and asserted by the people from different perspectives relevant to the successful implementation of the project. It is the responsibility of the project management team to coordinate and harness the inputs to the Work Plan.

Where there may be an element of the project of which there is no any member of the team with requisite capacity to examine, the team will do well to seek the input of an expert who will provide informed breakdown of the activities, the duration and cost. In this the way, the Work Plan can be very much enriched.

Time to Prepare the Plan

The time the Work Plan is prepared has an impact on the

usefulness of the document and invariably, the performance of the project. For most projects other than the initial Work Plan which captures the overall project and its duration, annual Work Plans are usually produced to cover activities scheduled within the year. It will not make sense to have the overall Work Plan prepared after the implementation of the project has commenced or the year has already started before the annual Work Plan is prepared and approved by the relevant authority. A plan produced in retrospect suggests that a time had been in the project when there was no plan. This will question the efficiency of the project management team. The right thing to do is to have the Work Plan prepared and approved way ahead of the commencement date for the implementation of the plan.

Information Required for the Preparation of the Plan

The Work Plan is a reflection of the project management teams' understanding of the requirements of the project. For most development agencies' supported projects, there are some basic documents that do provide the information that can enable a true understanding of the requirements upon which the Work Plan is based. These include:

- Project Appraisal Document;
- Financing Agreement;
- Operational Manual or Implementation Arrangement;
- Rules and Procedures for Procurement;
- Disbursement Guidelines;
- Aide Memoires;
- Project Related Studies; and
- Strategic Plan;

The totality of the information that these documents provide will make clear with respect to the project, the scope, quality, time and cost, and lead the team in the preparation of the Work Plan. Scope entails all the deliverables in form of products (works, goods), services and outcomes that all together upon realization constitute the completed project. A sense of quality is the perfect description and specification of the deliverables. Time indicates when part or all the deliverables ought to be delivered. Finally, cost relates to the budget for the project. It is when one is armed with this information and properly understands them along with the indicated constraints, rules and guidelines governing the operation of the project that an effective Work Plan can be developed.

Development of the Work Plan

The fundamental key to the preparation of Work Plan is the development of Work Breakdown Structure (WBS). The WBS is the division of the project into small elements as such that each of the element is an identifiable part of the project; manageable in the sense that the responsibility of undertaking it can be assigned to a person or entity; independent or loosely dependent on other ongoing elements; can be integrated harmoniously into the entire project; and measurable that its progress can be ascertained (**H. Kerzner, 2017**). In view of the role the WBS plays in developing a Work Plan, it must be established carefully. The fact is that if the project has to be decomposed with each element fulfilling the characteristics mentioned above, then perfect understanding of the project requirements and strong reasoning in terms of optimal process of achievement and resource needs are prerequisite. This is why many people and experts are needed to get involved.

When the work breakdown (activity and tasks) has successfully been established, assignments of responsibilities, scheduling and budgeting are the other stages of developing the Work Plan. One principle of assigning responsibility is to for each activity have the person in the right position in terms of authority, capacity and availability chosen for the responsibility. Scheduling demands that the activities are scheduled in a sequential order, duration assigned to each, and start and end dates are determined. Among the techniques in carrying out the scheduling exercise are the Gantt Chart and Critical Path Method. Depending on how conversant the team is with these techniques, a simpler Gantt Chart may be preferred as it is easier to understand by all. Budgeting, just as scheduling requires appreciation of all that is involved in undertaking an activity and estimating the cost. Budgeting is further discussed in another section of this book.

Constituent and Structure of Work Plan

A typical Work Plan for development agencies' supported projects have three parts namely, narrative summary; activities and implementation; and complementary documents.

- ***Narrative Summary***

This is the narrative part of the Work Plan that has the following subjects covered in brief:

- The context of the project;
- Project description;
- Overall project objectives;
- Specific project objectives;

- Project components; and
- Project key deliverables and expected results.

- ***Activities and the Implementation***

This part of the Work Plan is better produced in excel sheet. It has on the rows the activities and tasks as established in the Work Breakdown Structure and on the columns for each of the activities or tasks the following details:

- Objective;
- Target (the person or entity the activity is targeted at);
- Output;
- Expected outcome and output indicators;
- Time frame (duration – start and end dates);
- Procurement method;
- Responsible person or entity for the implementation;
- Action steps;
- Action status (implementation milestone);
- Budget;
- Expenditures milestone dates;
- Expenditure status;
- Risks and assumptions;

- ***Complementary Documents (Appendix)***

These are essential documents that are separately prepared and have the content feed into the activity implementation section of the Work Plan. The Work Plan therefore is not complete without them. These documents include:

i. **Activity Schedule:** This contains all the activities and the scheduling usually presented in a Gantt Chart.
ii. **Implementation Arrangement:** This document

discusses and gives details of the following:

- Guiding rules and regulations for the implementation of the project;
- Governance structure;
- Roles and Responsibilities;
- Procurement Procedures;
- Reporting;
- Approvals; and
- Auditing;

iii. **Budget:** The document provides the details of the budget for the activities and the timing of the expected expenditures.

iv. **Disbursement Plan:** When the inflows for financing of the project are expected from the financiers are indicated in the Disbursement Plan.

v. **Procurement Plan:** This document indicates the method of procurement for the project activities and timing of the processes associated with each.

vi. **Monitoring and Evaluation Plan:** Referring to the Result Framework of the project, the document set the expected results per time and when the check is supposed to take place (annually, quarterly, etc.).

vii. **Risk Management Plan:** This document contains all the risks identified that have potential to impede performance, and the planned actions to mitigate them.

viii. **Environment and Social Safeguard Plan:** Based on studies and observations, the document provides steps towards preventing or minimizing any likely adverse impact of the project on the environment and the community.

BUDGET

As part of the Work Plan, budget is the finalized cost estimates for the execution of the scheduled activities according to the Work Based Structure (WBS) of the project. Two sets of budgets are usual with projects. The first is the overall budget covering the entire activities and duration of the project. The second are the annual budgets that relate to exclusively the activities of the project scheduled in a given year. The essence of budgets is to provide in the project a means of:

- Resource allocation;
- Resource control;
- Coordination of activities;
- Communication of cost information;
- Motivation towards set targets; and
- Evaluation of managerial performance.

Focus of the Performance Auditor

In view of the major role budgets play in the management of projects, the performance auditor will usually pay much attention to the budgets knowing that their existence and level of utilization significantly impacts the performance of the project. In an expectation to see that the budgets are effectively serving the desirable purpose, the performance auditor as he carries out the assessment as regards to the budgets will strongly consider majorly the following:

i. Budget performance;
ii. Budgetary and cost controls;
iii. Budget at completion.

Budget Performance

As a first level of budget assessment, the performance auditor without having regard to the scheduled activities for the year and those indeed executed during the year, will check the proportion of the budget value for the year that was actually spent at the end of the year. For the time-phased budget of a year, the level of the disparity between the amount budgeted for the year and the amount spent for the year will indicate the nominal performance of the budget. While a small percentage disparity shows good performance, wide disparity shows poor performance. In a case where for the year, the actual expenditures were just a little proportion of the budgeted amount and the cause is not due to adverse exogenous environmental or social conditions, the performance auditor may deduce either one or more of the followings:

i. The project management team was over ambitious;
ii. The project management team had no good judgement of the activities the execution was possible during the year;
iii. The project management team had insufficient capacity to implement the plan;
iv. There was near frustration of the Work Plan due to delayed process approvals.

The second level of performance auditor's assessment of the time-phased budget is to determine the real performance. This is done by comparing the output delivered using the actual expenditure for the year with the output that the same value of expenditure was to produce based on the budget. In order words, the budget is flexed. As an illustration, supposing the budget for the year to train 100 people in a Short Course is $150,000 and at the end of the year 60 people were trained with $120,000, the flexed budget is (120,000/60)*100 = $200,000. Ordinarily when the, $120,000 is compared with $150,000, it appears the budget has performed well but when compared with the flexed budget, $200,000, the real performance is poor as the output of 100 that would have been achieved with $150,000 cannot be achieved at a cost less than $200,000 based on this management's performance.

Budgetary and cost controls

In an attempt to evaluate the practice of budgetary and cost controls in the project, the performance auditor will look out for the availability of project reports that are generated by Management Cost and Control System (MCCS) developed by the project management team. The MCCS is such that enables at any time the activities schedules, performance and cost status of the project to be known prompting continuous management decisions of consolidation or correction of favorable or adverse results respectively. These reports relate to the budget and include progress reports, status reports, projection reports and exceptional reports. Furthermore, these reports are actually products of variance analysis that 'involves comparing actual performance against plan, investigating the causes of the variance and taking corrective action to ensure that targets are achieved' **P. Collier, 2009.**

There are three key parameters in these reports that the performance auditor uses to compute some ratios that do enable him to make emphatic statements on his measure of the level of cost, budgetary, and schedule controls for a given planned period. As defined by **H. Kerzner, 2017**, these parameters are:

i. Budgeted Cost for Work Scheduled (BCWS) – This is the budget cost for all the activities scheduled for the period;
ii. Budget Cost for Work Performed (BCWP) – This is the budget cost equivalent of the activities performed during the period; and
iii. Actual Cost for Work Performed (ACWP) – This is the actual cost of the executed activities in the period.

With these parameters, the computations and interpretations of ratios associated with measure of either cost, or schedule controls are shown in *Table 2.* Indeed these ratios are sufficient to pass judgments on the cost control leading to budgetary control.

Table 2: Measures of Results of Budget Management Assessment (Turn at 90°)

SN	Ratios	Subject and Unit of Measurement	Formular = X	Possible Results (X)	Interpretation of Results	Summary of the prevailing condition
1.	Cost Variance (CV)	Cost status compared with budget ($)	BCWP – ACWP = X	(i) 'X' is negative	There is cost overrun.	Adverse
				(ii) 'X' is zero	The cost is exact with the budget.	Neutral
				(iii) 'X' is positive	The cost is below the budgeted.	Favorable
2.	Cost Variance Percentage (CVP)	Cost status compared with budget (%)	CV/ BCWP = X	'X' is negative	There is cost overrun; utilization of resources is inefficient.	Adverse
				'X' is zero	The cost is exact with the budget.	Neutral
				'X' is positive	The cost is below the budgeted; there is efficient use of the resources.	Favorable

SN	Ratios	Subject and Unit of Measurement	Formular = X	Possible Results (X)	Interpretation of Results	Summary of the prevailing condition
3.	Cost Performance Index (CVI)	Cost status compared with budget (%)	BCWP/ ACWP = X	'X' is less than 1.00	The activities are being achieved at extra cost above the budgeted; utilization of resources is inefficient.	Adverse
				'X' is 1.00	The cost is exact with the budget.	Neutral
				'X' is more than 1.00	The activities are being achieved at lower cost than the budgeted; there is efficient use of the resources.	Favorable
4.	Schedule Variance (SV)	Activities' progress compared with the scheduled in the Work Plan ($)	BCWP – BCWS = X	'X' is negative	The activities are running behind schedule.	Adverse
				'X' is zero	The achievement of the activities is exact with the schedules.	Neutral
				'X' is positive	More than the scheduled activities have been accomplished.	Favorable

SN	Ratios	Subject and Unit of Measurement	Formular = X	Possible Results (X)	Interpretation of Results	Summary of the prevailing condition
5.	Schedule Variance Percentage (SVP)	Activities' progress compared with the scheduled in the Work Plan (%)	SV/ BCWS = X	'X' is negative	The activities are running behind schedule.	Adverse
				'X' is zero	The achievement of the activities is exact with the schedules.	Neutral
				'X' is positive	More than the scheduled activities have been accomplished.	Favorable
6.	Schedule Performance Index (CVI)	Activities' progress compared with the scheduled in the Work Plan (%)	BCWP/ BCWS = X	'X' is less than 1.00	The activities are being achieved at a slower rate than the planned.	Adverse
				'X' is 1.00	The accomplishments are exact with the schedule.	Neutral
				'X' is more than 1.00	The activities are being achieved at a faster rate than the planned.	Favorable

Budget at Completion

The last of the issues the performance auditor would be concerned with on the budget is comparison of the already known project's Budget at Completion (BAC) with his computation of most reasonable cost estimate of the project at completion i.e. Estimate at Completion (EAC). As in the last section, the parameters the performance auditor uses to compute the EAC are the BCWS, BCWP and ACWP. These parameters are manipulated to carry out the calculation of the EAC depending on the following three mutually exclusive assumptions of the auditor:

i. At any given time, the projected final cost of the project is directly related to ratio of the actual cost of the executed work so far, to the budget provided for the same work. This ratio which is the burn rate will remain uniform and affect the outstanding works and the associated budget in the same manner as the observed with the executed;

   Here, EAC = (ACWP/BCWP) x BAC

ii. At any given time, the projected final cost of the project is directly related to ratio of the actual cost of the executed work so far, to the budget provided for the same work. However, while this ratio which is the burn rate is applicable to the completed and on-going works, the outstanding works will be completed at cost same as the associated budget;

   Here, EAC = [(ACWP/BCWP) x (Executed and on-going works)] + (Budget of outstanding works)

iii. At any given time, actual cost of the executed work so far neither relates to the budget provided for the same work nor the likely cost of the budgeted outstanding works.

Here, EAC = Actual cost of executed works + Budgets of balance of on-going works and fully outstanding works.

Based on the calculated EAC, and when it is compared with the BAC, the performance auditor will make assertions vis-à-vis budget performance and control on the likely cost overrun of the project or otherwise.

Preparation of Budget

Having understood the likely measures of assessment of the project management team's performance in dealing with its own budget, the preparation and management of the budget must be considered critical in order to path a course towards the auditor's commendation.

Preparation of project budget is an art that is made manifest if only the project management team:

- Have understanding of the project, its activities and the tasks;
- Have understanding of the drivers of costs in each activity or tasks;
- Have knowledge of past events and the impacts on performance; and
- Make reasonable assumptions and judgments regarding future events.

As always, the process of budgeting primarily includes

establishment of the Work Based Structure, estimating of the cost of the activities or tasks and allocation of resources in accordance with the strategic goals of the project – both short term and long run. Not neglecting any of the processes, the key aspect of budgeting in projects is estimation of costs in the order of the WBS. This demands capability and ability to forecast. Capability here may require technical capacity depending on the nature, size and complexity of specific elements of the project. For instance, for a project involving building infrastructure element, a quantity surveyor would be required to carry out the cost estimate that then will be incorporated in the budget. Regarding ability to forecast, having ascertained the cost drivers of the activities, the cost trend and the factors that affect the costs must be considered in arriving at the budget provision for each activity. Some of the common economic, social and environmental factors worth considering are inflation, exchange rate, labour unrest, political instability, climate, etc.

Overall, the cost estimates and necessary adjustments that together constitute the budget must be as realistic as possible. A low budget will put undue pressure on cash management leading to either forced reallocation of funds, search for alternative financing, frustration, or abandonment of some activities or the entire project. On the other hand, when the budgets are exaggerated, the adverse consequence may include recklessness in spending, lower measure of budget performance, and suspicion on extra judicial use of the provisions.

While preparing the budget, it is important for the purposes of evaluation of project performance and cost control in the future that the budget is structured to reflect (1) the core project activities, ancillary project activities, and administrative costs, and (2) the time phasing usually in terms of 1-year, half-year, quarters or monthly. Ancillary project activities are those that are incidental to the performance of the core project activities. For example, in a project to train students, the cost of the processes for the selection of the scholars may be considered ancillary. Administrative cost for instance where the project is domiciled in an agency will include direct staff cost, apportioned staff cost, operational cost, and institutional overheads. This arrangement of the budget as typified in *Table 3* enhances strategic allocation of funds, cost control and cash management – all towards the optimal accomplishment of the project goals.

Table 3: Typical Budget Structure

S/N	WBS – Groupings	Time – Phasing Budget			
		1-Year	Half-Year	Quarter(s)	Month(s)
A	Core Project Activities				
B	Ancillary Project Activities				
C	Administrative Costs				
	Total				

Management of Budget (Budgetary Control)

After the planning cycle of the project having the Work Plan and the time phased budget, the management of the budget or budgetary control requires that during the operating cycle of the project, the focus is to observe if there exist divergence between the planned and the actual, and make efforts to close the gap if any at minimal cost. Budgetary control primarily entails ensuring that the financial results in the course of the operation of the project are in line with the targets – both interim and final.

Effective budgetary control does not exist in a vacuum or by chance but through a developed system that serves as a feedback mechanism as it measures actual progress and cost, relate same with the planned and gives insight of the control required to narrow or zero the disparity. A good system should be such that the intervals of the feedback as the resources are employed into the project are very short to allow for early consolidation or corrective measures as the case may be. Realizing this control will require the project management team to continually carry out:

- Early accounting of actuals – progress and expenditures;
- Variance analysis;
- Re-estimation of completion time and cost at designated milestones of the project;

Variance Analysis

Variance analysis involves making comparison at a given time of the actual expenditures on specified works during a period with the planned, investigating reasons responsible for the variance if any, and taking actions to either correct adverse variances or consolidate favourable variances. Adverse variance occurs when the actual expenditure is higher than the budget. Favourable variance is when the actual expenditure is less than the budget.

Variance analysis is a basic technique for budgetary control. With a well-developed Work Plan indicating cost centers, the variance analysis is conducted on each of the WBS and a report produced for use in the cost control cum budgetary control decisions. A typical variance analysis report will contain the information shown in *Table 4*. The process of the preparation of the variance analysis poses some questions to the project management team that the answers help to retrace its steps and refocus its actions towards achieving the project objectives at the right time and cost. Some of these questions when variance is observed include:

- Is the variance significant as such that requires investigation?
- What are the current or potential impacts of the variance?
- What are the causes of the variance?
- Are the causes controllable?
- What are the possible actions to take to control or mitigate the impact of the variance?
- Who is in the best position to take the necessary actions and at what time?

With proper variance analysis and reporting at appropriate times in line with the time phased budget, it would be evident to the project management team when replanning is inevitable, and if done based on cost data collection and cost accounting performed in the past, a more assuring Estimate at Completion can be established and the control towards same enhanced.

Table 4: Typical Variance Analysis Structure (*Turn at 90°*)

Cost Code	WBS Element	BCWP	ACWP	Variance	Adverse/ Favourable	Variance Significant? (Yes/ No)	Reasons Responsible for Variance	Anticipated Impact	Lessons and/or Corrective Actions	Responsible for Actions

PROCUREMENT OF GOODS, WORKS AND SERVICES

With development agencies' funded programs like many others, procurement of goods, works and services play significant role in the performance of the project. Therefore, it is one aspect of the project management that the auditors will concentrate on while examining the performance of the project. The basis of assessment of the management of the procurements is centered on the extent to which the project management team in its implementation of the procurement processes is consistent with generally acceptable procurement objectives, principles and characteristics. In this regard, subjects of the assessment with respect to procurements under the project that the auditors would focus on normally shall include the:

- Planning and timeliness of the activities;
- Effectiveness, economy, and efficiency of the process;
- Transparency, fairness and integrity exercised in the process;
- Fit-for-purpose observed in the choice of procedures and processes;
- Level of documentation employed; and
- Anti-corruption observation.

Procurement Objective, Principles and Characteristics

At the core of every procurement should be the specific objective of that procurement in support of the overall goal of the project's objective. Next to the objective should be the principle to observe and finally, the characteristics embedded in or enclosing the procurement. This is represented diagrammatically in *Figure 2.* To appreciate these key issues of procurement, the European Bank for Reconstruction and

Development, World Bank Group and African Development Bank have provided in their respective procurement guidelines, epitomizing best practices, the expected universal procurement objective, principles and characteristics which are summarized as follows:

Figure 2: Objectives, Principles and Characteristics of Procurement

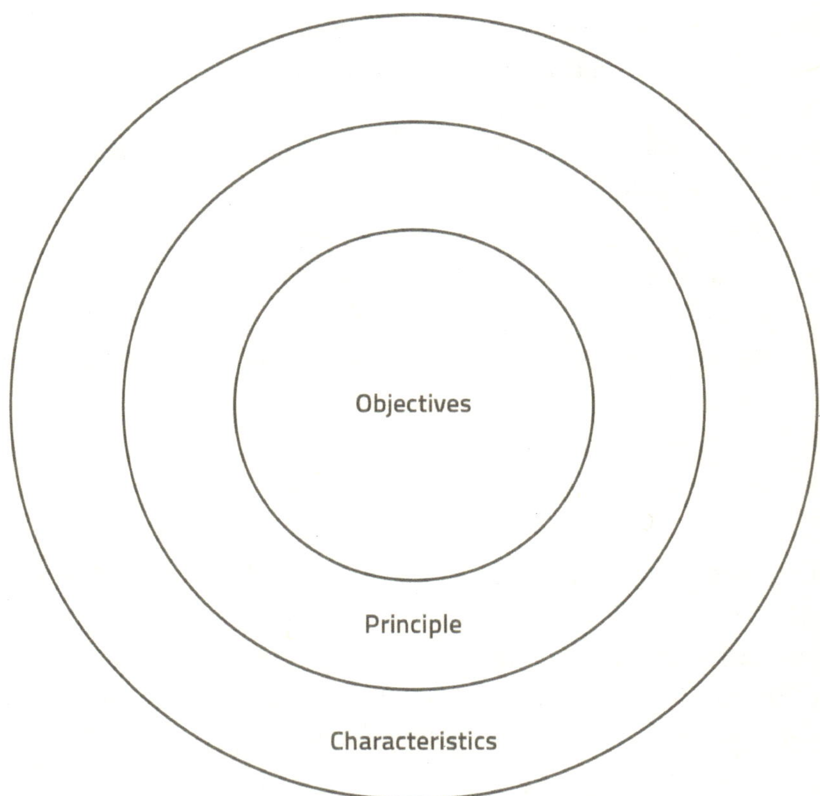

Objective

The objective of every procurement should always be to obtain the appropriate goods, works, services for the required purpose, at the required time and place, and for an appropriate cost, with due regard to the defined principles and characteristics of the process.

Principles

Value for Money (VfM):

The principle of procurement of goods, works and services is hinged on Value for Money condition. This is a state of having maximum benefits from each unit of resource spent with the purpose of achieving the project's objectives. This entails the effective, efficient, and economic use of resources, which requires an evaluation of relevant costs and benefits, along with an assessment of risks, and non-price attributes and/or life cycle costs, as appropriate. Price alone may not necessarily represent VfM.

Economy:

Economy is that measure of pricing of goods, works and/or services that expends the minimum quantum of resources to obtain an agreed level of output. For example, for a given goods on *Figure 3* wherein the vertical axis represents the prices ($) and the horizontal axis, the quantities (Q-kg), the curve, ('c') where the price is $25 and the quantity, 45kg is that with best economy among the three curves, 'a', 'b' and 'c.'

Figure 3: Economy in Procurements illustrated

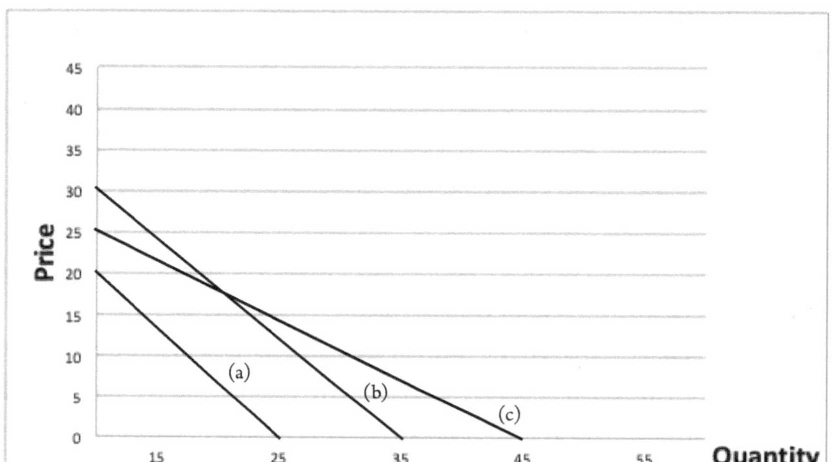

To ensure that economy is achieved in the procurement of an item as such to reasonably support value-for-money, strong considerations by the project management team need be given to the following costs for their optimization:

- Initial Cost of the item;
- Life Cycle Costs of the item – i.e costs relating to the usage of the item during its economic life (including operations, maintenance, insurance, storage, disposal and residual value);
- Cost of the transaction to the project (procuring entity);
- Cost of the transaction to bidders;
- Costs or benefits of the externalities (social and environmental factors etc.); and
- Costs of the conditions of contract that address specific risks (insurance, payment guarantee, performance security, etc).

Efficiency:

Efficiency in procurement entails the appropriate process management of a given quantum of resources to obtain an agreed level of output under a procurement process that ensures optimal VfM.

It requires that procurement processes be proportional to the value and risks of the underlying project activities. Sense of proportionality demands that the transaction and overhead costs; period of the process; and extent of mitigation of the prevailing risks are all reasonably related to the underlying project activity. The optimal relationship can be achieved by appropriate procurement skill, time management, internal structure, contract packaging, etc.

In simple term, efficiency entails realizing the most responsive outcome with the least amount of wasted effort or expense.

Effectiveness:

Effectiveness takes into account the contribution of the procurement process towards the accomplishment of the project objectives with respect to institutional or national economic, social, environmental development.

'Contribution' and 'accomplishment' are key words in effectiveness and are critical drivers in realizing VfM.

Characteristics

This refers to procedural actions associated with procurement that beyond the principle of economy, efficiency and effectiveness, the said procedural action are on the basis of, and indeed characterized by fairness, transparency, and integrity.

Fairness

Fairness is encapsulated in equal opportunity to and equal treatment of interested business seekers. Equal opportunity includes access to information and disclosure of evaluation criteria, terms and conditions of contract. Equal treatment relates to being impartial and non-discriminatory. Fairness is also seen when credible mechanisms for addressing procurement-related complaints are provided.

Transparency

Transparency requires that relevant procurement information is made publicly available to all interested parties, consistently and in a timely manner, through readily accessible and widely available sources at reasonable or no cost.

The act of transparency must be seen in four dimensions – availability, clarity and predictability.

- **Availability** requires that information during the procurement process for business seekers and information on the procurement for other stakeholders are available and accessible at reasonable cost post procurement activities;
- **Clarity** relates to precision and consistency in conveyance to interested stakeholders of procurement requirements as such that usual understanding of the document are not hindered;
- **Predictability** relates to level of certainty on the outcome of the process given the same conditions.

Integrity

Integrity entails absolute respect and commitment to one's

obligations and promises under the project, and most importantly to uphold at all times the project and public interests above personal and undue interest of any other.

For the WBG, it refers to the use of funds, resources, assets, and authority according to the intended purposes and in a manner, that is well informed, aligned with the public interest, and aligned with broader principles of good governance.

What this means is that all persons or entities playing a role in the procurement process from all the sides must exercise highest standard of ethics during the process. Fraud and corruption must not be practiced.

Procurement Methods and Fit-For-Purpose Concept

Procurement methods refer to the different methods employed in the process that leads to the award of contracts for provision of goods, works or services under the project. This process is broadly categorized into two, namely, open competitive and limited competitive - tender process. While in the open competitive, opportunity is granted to all interested entities enabling perfect competition, limited competitive have the participation restricted to limited number which sometimes may just be one thus, the competition is limited. The two processes can one at a time be employed in either national or international markets in which case the former has the participation exclusive to the entities within national geographical boundaries and the later, beyond the national boundaries. In either of the market approach, most development agencies will prefer open competitive tender process to limited competitive procurements in the project they support. The measure of preference is illustrated in *Figure*

4 below.

Figure 4: Scale of preference of procurement methods

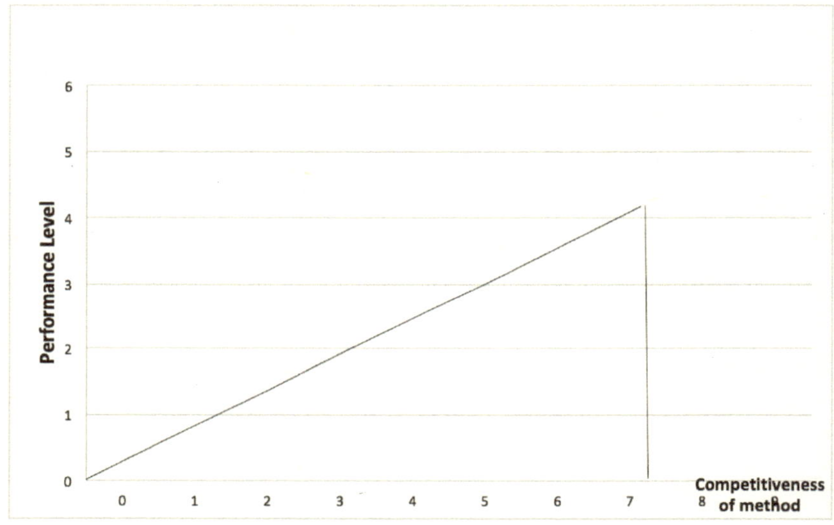

However, without prejudice to the scale of preference in terms competitiveness of the tender process, there are other factors that may be considered in deciding the procurement method to adopt at a time. Generally, with respect to an expected project output, procurement methods depend on:

- Category - goods, works or services
- Size
- Complexity
- Delivery Time
- Source
- Risk

The different procurement methods and the basic procedures of each are contained in *Table 6.* The aim of choosing a particular method at a time is to have the process and outcome optimally contribute to the project development objectives and outcomes. The fit-for-purpose concept of procurement is a function of the choices being made on procurement method and its suitability and reasonability under a particular circumstance. In totality, fit-for-purpose consideration entails the combined choices of the procurement method and market approach to achieve the core principles of procurement – value for money, economy, efficiency, effectiveness and equity. For guidance, the **World Bank Group** has indicated the circumstances wherein each procurement method and the market approach are most suitable. These are summarized in *Tables 5 and 6.*

Table 5: Procurement Market Approach and Conditions for Application (Turn at 90°)

Community	Conditions	Competitiveness	Conditions
National	Where the value, size and conditions of contract are not such that can ordinarily attract international entities' participation and there is sufficient capability locally to meet the Project's requirement.	Open	• Where highest competition is required thus without restriction, all eligible and interested entities are given equal opportunity to participate.
		Limited	• Where only limited number of firms are capable of meeting Project's requirements or other justifiable reasons exist.
		Sole	• Where continuation of existing contract is required; • Where there is need to replicate completed contracts successfully performed within the last 12 months • Where only one provider exists • For items of very low value with low risk; • For emergency situation.
International	In a case of complex, high risk and/or high value contracts where international entities' participation will further guarantee desired contract performance.	Open	As in 'National' above
		Limited	As in 'National' above
		Sole	As in 'National' above

Table 6: Procurement Methods and Conditions for Application (Turn at 90°)

S/N	Procurement Methods	Basic Process	Conditions
A. GOODS, WORKS AND NON-CONSULTING SERVICES			
1A.	Request for Proposals (Two-Stages Model)	The process consists of Initial Selection plus two other stages. The Initial Stage involves release of Specific Procurement Notice through Newspapers and approved online medium after which selection based on set criteria is made from the received applications. These selected applicants are issued Request for Proposals of which only Technical Proposals are received and evaluated. The successful applicants thereafter make detailed Technical Proposal accompanied with Financial Proposal. The Financial Proposal is opened at a later date in public and based on the combined evaluation of both the Technical and Financial Proposals, the choice of the Most Advantageous Proposals is made.	Where due to the nature and complexity, there is no clarity or certainty in the manner the Project's requirement can be best met. In such cases, participants are given the opportunity to offer customized solutions to satisfy the requirement.

S/N	Procurement Methods	Basic Process	Conditions
1B.	Request for Proposals (Streamlined Model)	The process consists of Initial Selection plus one other stage. The Initial Stage involves release of Specific Procurement Notice through Newspapers and approved online medium after which selection based on set criteria is made from the received applications. These selected applicants are issued Request for Proposals. Both Technical and Financial Proposals are received at the same time though the Financial Proposal is opened at a later date in public. Upon completion of the combined evaluation of Technical and Financial Proposals, the Most Advantageous Proposal is identified and subsequently subjected to post-qualification. Only if the identified Most Advantageous Proposal fails in the post-qualification will the next in rank tested in its qualifications.	Where due to the nature and complexity, there is no clarity or certainty in the manner the Project's requirement can be best met. In such cases, participants are given the opportunity to offer customized solutions to satisfy the requirement.

S/N	Procurement Methods	Basic Process	Conditions
1C.	Request for Proposals (Competitive Dialogue)	The process consists of Initial Selection plus rounds of dialogues. The Initial Stage involves release of Specific Procurement Notice through Newspapers and approved online medium after which selection based on set criteria is made from the received applications. These selected applicants (not less than three but not more than six) are issued Request for Proposals. Upon receipt of draft Technical Proposals from all, each is confidentially engaged in a dialogue that continues until the considered draft Technical Proposals are reduced to a number not less than three. These remaining applicants are requested to submit final Technical Proposals that invariably marks the end of the dialogue process. The final Technical Proposal received along with the Financial Proposal are jointly evaluated to determine the Most Advantageous Proposal.	Where due to the nature and complexity of requirement, the Project is unable to realistically define technical or performance specifications, and/or most suitable legal and financial framework except supports through discussions with the would-be providers are received

S/N	Procurement Methods	Basic Process	Conditions
2A.	Request for Bids [One Envelope Process (Without Pre-qualification)]	The process starts with the issuance of Specific Procurement Notice through Newspapers and approved online medium. Subsequently, all interested entities are enabled to obtain the Request for Bids. Upon receipt of the submitted Request for Bids comprising of both technical and financial parts in a single envelope, evaluation is carried out based on the set criteria to determine the Most Advantageous Bid. As part of the evaluation process, the Most Advantageous Bid is further subjected to post-qualification test. Only if this top Most Advantageous Bid fails in the technical post-qualification will the next ranked be tested similarly.	The project is capable and do indeed define and specify its requirements as such that the Bidders on their parts simply offer bids.

S/N	Procurement Methods	Basic Process	Conditions
2B.	Request for Bids [Two Envelope Process (Without Pre-qualification)]	The process starts with the issuance of Specific Procurement Notice through Newspapers and approved online medium. Subsequently, all interested entities are enabled to obtain the Request for Bids. Upon receipt of the submitted Request for Bids comprising of both technical and financial parts packaged in two different envelopes, evaluation of the technical part is carried out based on the set criteria. The result of the technical evaluation is communicated to the bidders with a date fixed for the public opening of the financial part. Based on the combined evaluation of the technical and financial parts, the Most Advantageous Bid is identified and further subjected to post-qualification test. Only if this top Most Advantageous Bid fails in the technical post-qualification will the next ranked be tested similarly.	The project is capable and do indeed define and specify its requirements as such that the Bidders on their parts simply offer bids.

S/N	Procurement Methods	Basic Process	Conditions
3.	Request for Quotation	The process starts with the issuance of Specific Procurement Notice through Newspapers and approved online medium. Subsequently, all interested entities are enabled to obtain the Request for Quotation. Those received through the specified means are evaluated in accordance with the criteria set in the Request for Quotations. Conclusively, the lowest evaluated quotation is accepted.	Where the subject of procurement is either off-the-shelf items, standardized specification commodities, or simple civil work; all small quantities and value
4.	Direct Selection	The process is based on the circumstance warranting the choice for sole selection.	Suitable for: • continuation of existing contract; • replication of completed contracts successfully performed within the last 12 months • items of very low value with low risk • only one provider exists • emergency situation
Related Procurement Arrangement			
5.	E-Revers Auction	The same process as in Request for Quotations except that it is electronically automated.	It is a form of RFQ and so the same conditions apply.

S/N	Procurement Methods	Basic Process	Conditions
6.	Commodities	The same process as Request for Bids [One Envelope – Without Pre-qualification] except that the participating bidders are mainly public sector entities.	Where continuous supply of a commodity at such intervals that will keep the inventories low is required. To achieve this, either multiple awards are made for supply of portions of the entire quantities at times that also take advantage of favourable market conditions. Examples of commodities include grain, oil, fertilizer, etc
7.	Community-driven Development	The process is as applicable in either Request for Bids or Request for Quotation, except that it is localized in a community.	Where local participation in the supply or implementation of part of the project will promote sustainability, advance local know-how and absorb excess available labour

S/N	Procurement Methods	Basic Process	Conditions
8.	Force Accounts	The process is dependent on the internal procedures of the executing agency.	Where inevitably the only practical way of carrying out the supply of Goods or execution of works is by the employment of the in-house resources – personnel and plants. Such circumstance may include: • the works are small and scattered in different locations that will not be attractive to contractors • the works cannot be easily defined and probably if were to be performed by the contractor will entail using 'dayworks'. • Required urgent repairs to halt further deterioration • Matters of security that it will be inappropriate for external entities to be involved in the supply or works.

S/N	Procurement Methods	Basic Process	Conditions
B. CONSULTING SERVICES			
9.	Quality and Cost-based Selection (QCBS)	The real process starts with the Shortlist created thus: As the Request for Expression of Interest is issued through Newspapers and approved online medium, the prepared Terms of Reference is made available to interested entities. Based on the Expression of Interest received and evaluated in accordance with the Terms of Reference, a Shortlist is created and approved for participation in the subsequent stages of the process. Letters of Invitation to Submit Proposals are sent to the entities in the Shortlist. Upon receipt of the Proposals which are in two parts, Technical and Financial contained in different envelopes, the Technical part is evaluated first based on the set criteria, and the result communicated to all that made submission. Those that met the minimum required score are informed to be present at the public opening of only their Financial Proposals. The combined evaluation of the Technical and Financial Proposals recognizing the assigned weights as contained in the Request for Proposal, the Most Advantageous Proposal is determined. Negotiation is then carried out with this top Most Advantageous Proposal and except if the negotiation fails would the next ranked be invited for similar negotiation.	Among the Shortlist, consideration is given to the quality of the Proposal and cost of the services. The sum of the two based on the weights assigned to each determines the Most Advantageous Proposal
10.	Fixed Budget-based Selection (FBS)		Exact consideration as QCBS but with a fixed budget that must not be exceeded. This is most suited for simple and well-defined assignment of which the budget can be reasonably estimated as a cost sufficient for a reasonable Proposer to carry out the assignment
11.	Least Cost-based Selection (LCS)		Exact consideration as in QCBS but least cost is singly prioritized after grouping of the top-quality Technical Proposals. This is appropriate for simple and standard or routine nature assignment. For example, audit of small progress.

S/N	Procurement Methods	Basic Process	Conditions
12.	Quality-based Selection	Letters of Invitation to Submit Proposals are sent to the entities in the Shortlist created as above. Upon receipt of the Proposals which are in two parts, Technical and Financial contained in different envelopes, the Technical part is evaluated first based on the set criteria, and the result communicated to all that made submission. On the date set for opening the Financial Proposals, only that of the entity with the highest technical score is opened. Evaluation of the opened Financial Proposal is then carried out and afterwards followed with negotiation.	Here cost is not an evaluation criterion but exclusively quality. The method is best used where the required assignment is highly specialized; can be carried out in substantially different ways which also abnitio cannot be precisely defined.
13.	Consultant's Qualification-based Selection	The Shortlist is not created as above but by discretionary limited selection not exceeding three. The Terms of Reference and Request for Expression of Interest are sent to them basically requiring that they give detailed information on their capacity. Upon evaluation of the submissions according to the set criteria, the one with the highest experience and most qualifications is invited to submit Technical and Financial Proposals concurrently. Following the evaluation of the proposals, negotiation is carried out to conclude the process.	It is limited competitive procurement where only selected few are given the opportunity to submit Expression of Interest. The most qualified is invited to submit both technical and financial proposals. This is most suitable for small assignments or Emergency Situation

S/N	Procurement Methods	Basic Process	Conditions
14.	Direct Selection	The process is based on the circumstance warranting the choice for sole selection.	Suitable for: • continuation of existing contract; • replication of completed contracts successfully performed within the last 12 months • items of very low value with low risk • when only one provider exists • emergency situation
Related Procurement Arrangement			
15.	Individual Consultant	The processes employed in all of the above methods are applicable except that rather than firms, individuals are the participants.	Where a team of experts is not required, and an individual can practicably carry out the assignment.
16.	UN Agencies	The process is based on the circumstance warranting the choice for a UN Agency selection.	Where UN Agency can provide technical assistant and advisory services in the area of their expertise, they can be directly selected particularly in Emergency Situation or capacity dearth.

S/N	Procurement Methods	Basic Process	Conditions
17.	Non-profit Organization	The process is based on the circumstance warranting the choice for the inclusion of non-profit organization in the selection.	An NGO based on their unique qualification and/or experiences in the community of their operations can be included in the Shortlist to participate in the contract procurement process

Procurement Planning and Timeliness

As required in all aspects of project management, planning is key to the pillars of quality, cost and time. In the context of procurements, Procurement Plan is an essential document that the performance auditors would be interested firstly in confirming the existence, and then follow up with an assessment of the quality, implementation, and timeliness of execution of the plan. Most development agencies will require for their projects that the Procurement Plan covers an initial period of eighteen months beginning from the start of the project, and subsequently, twelve months periods.

With the objective of supporting the project's objectives and value-for-money, some of the critical factors that can enable the project management team prepare high quality Procurement Plan includes:

i. Understanding of the project documents – Project Appraisal Report, Finance Agreement, etc.;

ii. Identification of the potential contracts by their nature, size, complexity, delivery time, risks, etc.

iii. Excellent understanding of the different procurement methods and the matching fit-for-purpose;

iv. Understanding of the required approval stages and processes associated with the procurement processes;

Having these understanding, a typical Procurement Plan will have among other content information on the followings with respect to each of the identified potential contracts:

- Procurement Method;
- Pricing and Costing Mechanism (Lumpsum, Cost-Plus, Performance Contract, etc);

- Estimated Cost;
- Review and Approval Requirements (Prior, Post, etc)
- Time Schedule of Process Activities (Invitation, Submission, Evaluation, etc)

All of this information as expected in the Procurement Plan should be carefully provided and taken very seriously by the project management team since the Performance Auditor visiting later is likely to compare them with the recorded actual situation. Without ignoring others, most critical is the time schedule of the process activities. A high percentage of variance of dates of actual from the planned may indicate lack of capacity to manage the procurement processes and disregard for time that impact significantly on the performance of the project. For reference purpose, following the prescribed rules by most of the Development Agencies, the time period within which the procurement activities ought maximally to be completed for the different procurement methods requiring prior reviews are indicated in *Tables 7, 8, 9 and 10.*

Table 7: Activity Timeline for 'Request for Proposal (Two Stage Model Following Initial Selection)'

Activity	**Days**
Preparation of Initial Selection Document	14
Approval of the Initial Selection Document	7
Advertisement – Submission and Opening	30
Evaluation of submissions for Initial Selection	14
Approval of Initial Selection Report	7
Preparation of Request for Proposal	21
Approval of Request for Proposal Document	7
Submission of Request for Proposal – Technical Proposal (Initial)	30
Evaluation of Initial Technical Proposal	14
Approval of Technical Proposal Evaluation Report (Initial)	7
Submission of Final Technical Proposal and Financial Proposal	30
Evaluation of Final Technical Proposal	14
Approval of Technical Proposal Evaluation Report (Final)	7
Opening and Evaluation of Financial Proposal	7
Request for Best and Final Offer (BAFO)	3
Report of Probity	3
Approval of Probity Report	3
Standstill Period and Debriefing	25
Award of Contract	1
TOTAL	**244**

Table 8: Activity Timeline for 'Request for Bids [One Envelope Process (Without Pre-qualification)]'

Activity	**Days**
Preparation of Bid Document	30
Approval of the Bid Document	14
Advertisement – Submission and Opening of Bids	30
Evaluation of Bids	21
Approval of Bid Evaluation Report	14
Standstill Period and Debriefing	25
Award of Contract	1
TOTAL	**135**

Table 9: Activity Timeline for 'Consulting Services (QCBS, FBS, LCS, QBS)'

Activity	**Days**
Preparation of TOR for Shortlisting	14
Approval of the TOR for Shortlisting	7
Advertisement – Submission and Opening of Expression of Interest	10
Evaluation of Expression of Interest	14
Approval of Shortlist	7
Preparation of Request for Proposal	21
Approval of Request for Proposal Document	7
Submission of Request for Proposal	**21**
Evaluation of Technical Proposal	21
Approval of Technical Proposal Evaluation Report	7
Invitation for opening of Financial Proposal	7
Evaluation of Financial Proposal	14
Approval of Most Advantageous Proposal	7
Invitation for Negotiation	5
Approval of Negotiation	3
Standstill Period and Debriefing	25
Award of Contract	1
TOTAL	**191**

Table 10: Activity Timeline for 'Consulting Services (Consultant Qualification Based Selection)

Activity	**Days**
Preparation of TOR for Shortlisting	14
Approval of the TOR for Shortlisting	7
Advertisement – Submission and Opening of Expression of Interest	10
Evaluation of Expression of Interest	14
Approval of Shortlist	7
Preparation of Request for Proposal	21
Approval of Request for Proposal Document	7
Submission of Request for Proposal	**21**
Evaluation of Technical and Financial Proposals	21
Approval of Most Advantageous Proposal	7
Invitation for Negotiation	5
Approval of Negotiation	3
Standstill Period and Debriefing	25
Award of Contract	1
TOTAL	**163**

In view of the role procurement plays in the performance of projects, the project management team more than producing the plan also needs to track the activities in order to regularly have a self-audit in this regard. The World Bank Group has developed an online platform for effecting this most needed tracking of procurement activities in its projects. The tool, known as 'Systematic Tracking and Exchanges in Procurement (STEP)', not only facilitate the preparation of the Procurement Plan but enables tracking and updating of the plan as the actual dates of execution of the activities are inputted. When used, the output instantly exposes the performance of the project which then helps the management team to make amendments where necessary and not wait for the auditors.

Evaluations of Proposals and Bids

Still concerned with the essence of keeping to time in the management of the procurement processes, the evaluation of the proposals and bids submitted is a factor that may mar smooth approvals associated with the processes and slow down the entire performance of both procurements and the project at large. It is therefore pertinent that the project management team exhibit sufficient knowledge and capacity, and carry out the evaluations in appropriate manner to avoid incessant reviews or decline of approvals from the relevant authorities.

The process of Proposals or Bid evaluations starts with constitution of Evaluation Committee. It is advisable that the membership of the Committee should include at least one with expertise in an area relevant to the subject of procurement and another with financial knowledge. As much as possible ulterior motives in the appointment of persons into the committee should be avoided.

One major characteristic of good evaluation is that it is based exclusively on the criteria clearly stated in the Requests for Expression of Interest, Proposals or Bids. No other factors, methods or criteria other than that specified earlier should be employed in the evaluation of these submissions, else, the outcome would be suspicious and may not receive the desired approval. The process of evaluation as indicated in the issued requests must also be respected. Most likely considerations and flow that are typical of the evaluation processes for Request for Proposals and Request for Bids in development agencies' projects are shown in ***Figures 6 and 7*** respectively. A project management team that follows this pattern and strictly report accordingly sure will not miss the mark. Reporting, i.e. the Evaluation Report is as important as the evaluation process itself and must rest on the following three fundamental principles when being produced:

- It must be concise
- It must reflect the logical sequence of the evaluation process
- It must avoid conditional recommendation for the award of contract

Figure 5: Evaluation Process Flow for 'Request for Proposals' *(Turn at 90°)*

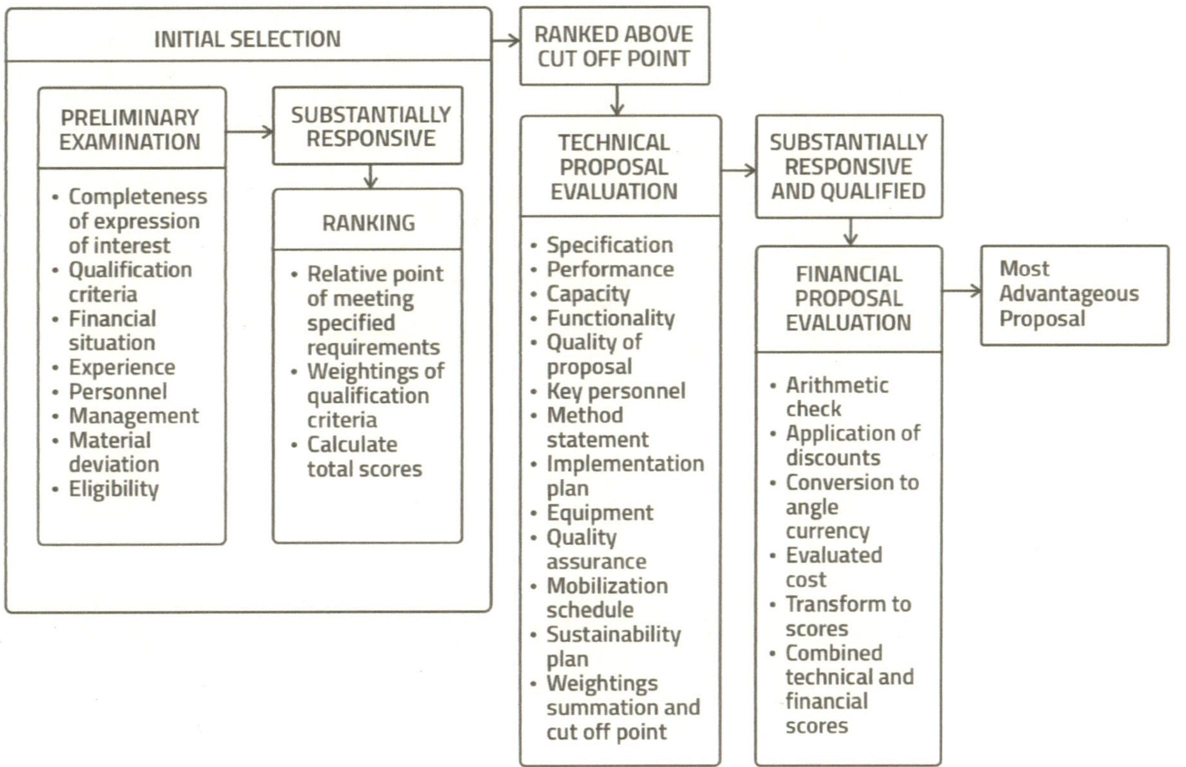

Figure 6: Evaluation Process Flow for 'Request for Bids'
(Turn at 90°)

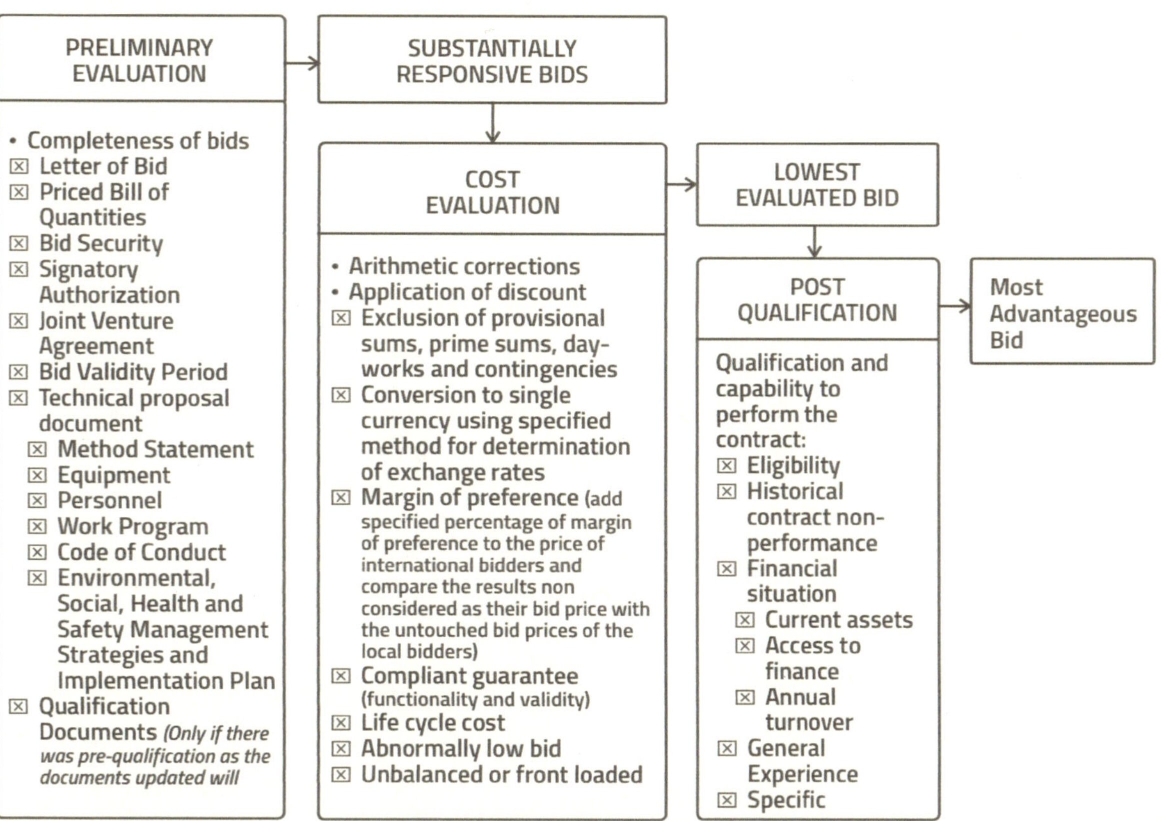

Notes:

- A bid/proposal is considered substantially responsive if it does not contain any major deviations from the bidding/proposal documents with regards to the validity of the bids and the commercial and technical conditions of the bids.

- The Most Advantageous Bid/Proposal is the Bid/Proposal that meets the qualification criteria and has been determined to be substantially responsive to the request for bids/request for proposals document; and is also the highest ranked Proposal or Bid with lowest evaluated cost.

CONTRACT MANAGEMENT

Among the key subjects of assessment of performance of a project is the output of the project. For most projects, significant portion of the outputs are realized through contract delivery hence the underlying interest of the performance auditor as he carries out his assignment is the level of successes or failures of the contracts under the project. Indeed, the success or failure of a contract performance is directly related to the performance of the contract management. This therefore makes contract management a focus of the performance auditor necessitating that the project management team be aware of and conducts its duties appropriately and deliberately as such to receive high approval of the auditors. Contract management is generally accepted as the art and science of managing a contractual agreement throughout the contractual process. For the practice to significantly impact the performance of the project positively, the disposition of the project management team in this regard must be founded on its:

- Appreciation of the purpose and scope of contract management;
- Understanding of the various types and suitability of contracts; and

- Development and implementation of Contract Management Plan.
- These also are the key issues that the performance auditor would be concerned with:

Purpose and Characteristics of Contract Management

The purpose of contract management is to create and maintain a drive leading to each party engaging its equipment, personnel and expertise effectively and efficiently, and in compliance to the agreed manner and conditions deliver the expected results of the contract.

Based on this purpose, some of the characteristics of contract management are that:

- It has aims;
- There is a drive towards the aims;
- Two parties or more are involved;
- Each party involved employs its resources;
- The manner and conditions of engagement of the resources are as agreed; and
- Expected results are delivered.

Unlike most other aspects of project management that the project management team solely undertakes, contract management goes beyond them to include the Contractor/ Supplier/Consultant to form the contract management team. This therefore makes it germane that the project management team be concerned with the happenings around and within the contractor's organization since though contract management is a collective responsibility, the performance auditor is more likely to focus on the roles and involvement of the project management team.

Types of Contracts

The place to begin contract management is to understand the various types of contracts and the suitability of each given different circumstances. *Table 11* provides a catalogue of commonly used contract types for a guide as the characteristics, advantages and disadvantages are indicated.

Table 11: Types of Contract – characteristics, advantages and disadvantages (*Turn at 90°*)

Types of Contracts	Core Characteristics	Conditions for Application	Advantages	Disadvantages
Lump Sum Contract (Fixed Price)	1. The contract amount is fixed; 2. Interim payments are made based on value of works executed and/ or contractual milestones	1. The scope of works can be clearly and accurately specified; 2. Interim payments can be directly linked to performance	1. Contractor undertakes to deliver the entire and completed works; 2. There is reasonable assurance of the ultimate cost; 3. Contractor assumes a large risk; 4. Owner is reasonably protected on the ultimate cost	1. Long period of preparation and adjudication of bids; 2. When there is inevitable need for change, in the specification, it creates some problems.

Types of Contracts	Core Characteristics	Conditions for Application	Advantages	Disadvantages
Unit Price (Admeasurement or Schedule of Rates)	1. The quantities of the items in the contract are estimated but not contractually binding; 2. The unit price of each of the included items is contractual and will be used to arrive at the item cost during the contract when the actual quantity is established.	1. When the nature of the contract is well defined, but the quantities of the items cannot be determined prior to the contract; 2. Used in maintenance or repair contracts; 3. Suitable for urgent works; 4. Where in the case of Goods and Non-Consulting Services, the quantity of the goods are known and the unit price is being sought from bidders.	1. Procurement preparation takes less time;	1. When an item occurs during the contract that is not included in the schedule of rates, the determination of the unit price may be problematic; 2. Absence of reasonable competitiveness as regards the adoption of a unit price for items not included in the schedule of rates.

Types of Contracts	Core Characteristics	Conditions for Application	Advantages	Disadvantages
Performance Based	**1.** Clear definition of a series of objectives and indicators by which to measure contractor performance; **2.** Payments are not made for inputs but for measured outputs that aim at satisfying functional needs in terms of quality, quantity, and reliability **3.** Contractor's performance may attract rewards or sanctions as the case may be.	1. Where the procurement objectives are better defined in terms of function; 2. Suitable for delivering public services; 3. Operation of facility to be paid on the basis of functional performance; 4. Also good for continuation of contract of defined functional output;	1. It is straight forward and easy to understand; 2. It can be scaled up or down easily (though within economic limits)	1. Interpretation and measure of functional performance may not be accurate; 2. Incentives may be perverted.

Types of Contracts	Core Characteristics	Conditions for Application	Advantages	Disadvantages
Reimbursable Cost-Plus Fee	1. The contractor is obliged to undertake the works at real cost and get reimbursed and paid an agreed fee to cover his overhead and profit; 2. The cost may vary but the fee remains fixed; 3. Contractor agrees to use his best efforts to perform the work.	1. When accurate pricing of the items cannot be achieved any other way; 2. Appropriate for emergency repairs and maintenance work.	1. The bidding document can be prepared easily; 2. When incentives are associated with the fees, value for money is further assured; 3. Provides maximum flexibility to owner.	1. Appropriate budgeting and planned financing may be difficult as final cost is lately determined; 2. Permit excessive change of design and/or specification by owner.

Types of Contracts	Core Characteristics	Conditions for Application	Advantages	Disadvantages
Time Based	1. The contract payment is determined by the application of agreed rates for time spent on the assignment; 2. Expenses incurred in the course of the assignment is reimbursed.	1. Emergency Situations, and repairs and maintenance work; 2. Consulting Services, when it is difficult to define or fix the scope and duration of the services.	1. It is easier to initiate.	2. Items of cost that are reimbursable may not be easily interpreted and measured; 3. Time determination may be marred with falsehood.
Turnkey	1. The Contractor undertakes the responsibility of the design through completion and commissioning; 2. The owner primarily receives the completed works and "turns the key".	1. Where high level of expertise is required but the providers are not much available; 2. In a case where monopoly exist with regards to the expected project output; 3. In emergency.	1. Less procurement preparation is required; 2. There is reasonable assurance of performance	1. Cost of the project may be unreasonably high and such that negates value for money

Strategy and Scope of Contract Management

A simple strategy of contract management is having to earnestly and in detail answer the direct five questions beginning with letter 'W' (5Ws) plus another two starting with letter 'H' (2Hs); all in relation to the contract. The 5Ws formulated by **Josephs and Rubenstein, 2018** are 'Why', 'What', 'When' 'Who', and 'Why Not', and the 2Hs, 'How', 'Have'. The network of these 'Ws' and 'Hs' that can be developed to form the contract management strategy is illustrated in *Figure 7*.

Figure 7: Strategic questions for Contract Management practice

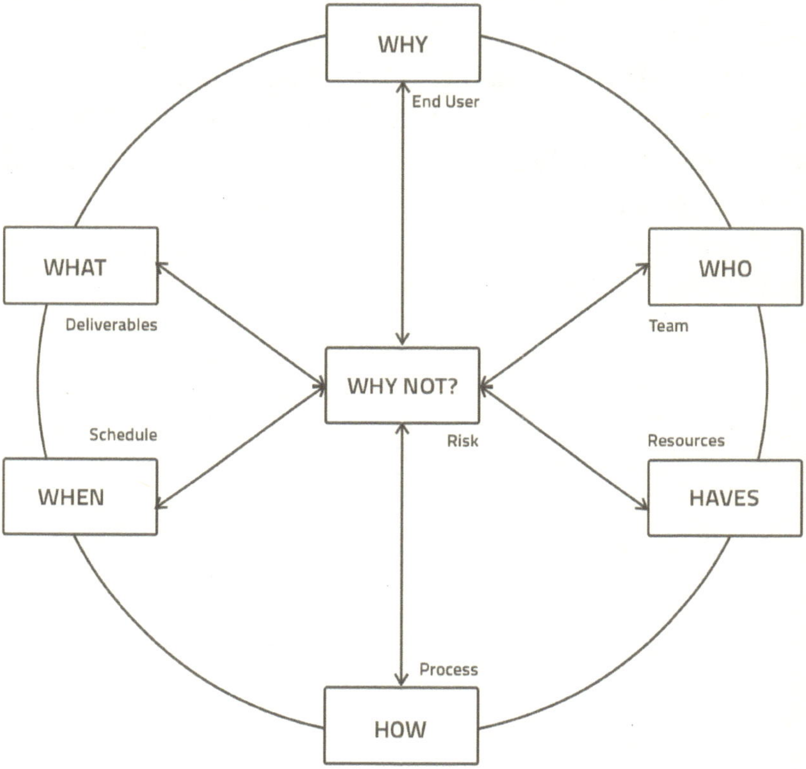

WHY:

Why is the contract being embarked upon; Probably there are needs that the output and outcome of the contract are meant to satisfy; Will the people facing the need get the expected satisfaction.

WHAT:

What are the deliverables of the contract; What values (tangible and intangible) is the contract supposed to create;

Specificity is required here.

WHEN:
When will these deliverables be delivered? Is it all at the end or some at some time and if so, when?

HOW:
How are the deliverables going to be accomplished? What are the processes and procedures and terms and conditions of getting things done?

HAVES:
What are the resources required to achieve the deliverables? Are they sufficiently in terms of quantity and quality available?

WHO:
Who are the ones going to make all of these happen? Is the team in place? Who are the members of the team and what role does each has to play?

WHY NOT:
Why not the end users get satisfaction, deliverables made and as scheduled too, process followed, resources available and right people available and doing what they are supposed to do. This "why not" question is all about risk – possible uncertain events that can stop the planned and expected from happening.

It is upon giving deep thoughts to these questions that the scope of contract management is revealed. As an art and science, contract management targets the manipulation of five subjects in other to realize the contract's objectives. These subjects grouped in three orbits are People, Time and Cost in the external orbit, Risk in the middle, and Deliverables at the core as shown in *Figure 8.*

Figure 8: Targets of management for contract delivery

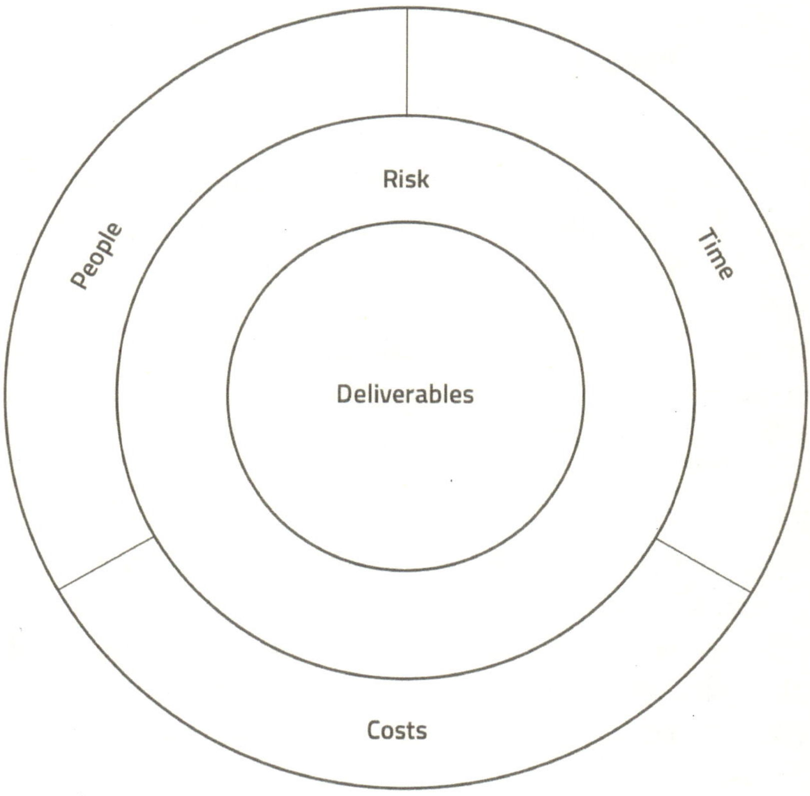

The specific considerations in the handling of these subjects in pursuit of effective and efficient contract management are contained in *Table 12.* These are also likely to form the basis of the assessment of contract management by the performance auditors.

Table 12: Assessment criteria for the targets of contract management

Targets of Contract Management	Specific Consideration	Brief of the Consideration
People	Capacity	The qualifications of the people vis-à-vis the functions they are expected to perform.
	Number	Are the number of qualified people sufficient for the volume of work associated with their functions?
	Availability	Although the records may show that a good number of persons engaged are qualified, are there evidence that they have also been available as the job demands.
	Commitment	What is the commitment level of the people with respect to their individual functions?

Targets of Contract Management	Specific Consideration	Brief of the Consideration
Time	Start Date	How does the actual start date of scheduled activities relate to the planned? How much of distortions to the milestone and completion dates are caused by irregular start date of the various activities?
	Milestone Dates	Are milestone dates for the completion of some activities adhered to; Are there special efforts towards meeting the milestone date even when there has been late start date of preceding activities? What is the impact of non-adherence?
	Completion Dates	Are completion dates of the activities and/or the project adhered to; Are there special efforts towards meeting the completion date even when there has been late start date of preceding activities? What is the impact of non-adherence?

Targets of Contract Management	Specific Consideration	Brief of the Consideration
Cost	Contract Price	Has the contract price remained the target at completion? How do the actual differ from the original price?
	Estimated Contract Cost	How frequent is the estimated contract cost varied adversely?
	Variations	What is the quantum, frequency and value of the variations introduced in the contract?
	Economic Environment	How is the protectionist response to the envisaged and/or prevailing economic environment?

Targets of Contract Management	**Specific Consideration**	**Brief of the Consideration**
Deliverables	Quantity	What is the quantity of the deliverables with respect to the contract?
	Quality	What is the quality of the deliverables with respect to the contract?
	Specification	How clear are the specifications made? Are they updated as to remain relevant and efficient in terms of life cycle cost?
	Fit for Purpose	Are both the quantity and quality of the deliverables at the time of delivery still relevant and have the potential to serve the purpose they are meant to serve?
Risk	People, Time, Cost, Deliverables	How are risk identified and mitigated or eliminated in order to have the impact of efficient management of people, time and cost lead to effective deliverables.

Contract Management Plan

The primary evidence of an attempt by the project management team to exercise effective contract management of the contracts under the project is the existence of a Contract Management Plan for each of the contracts. The performance auditor will strongly desire to see this. Where Contract Management Plan exists, it serves as an instrument of guidance, control, monitoring and evaluation of the performance of the contract. Indeed, for the performance auditor, the content and implementation of this document fully form the basis of the assessment of the performance of the contracts and by extension, significantly, the project.

A typical Contract Management Plan will have seven parts as follows:

Part 1: Contract Objectives
Part 2: Schedule of Works and Cash Flow
Part 3: Roles and Responsibilities
Part 4: Communication and Reporting
Part 5: Critical Contract Terms and Conditions
Part 6: Risks and Mitigation
Part 7: Contract Management Performance Framework and Measurement

Part 1: Contract Objectives

Under this part, the objective of the contract is stated, and the key contract deliverables and performance indicators are identified. The key contract deliverables should be in terms of quantity, quality and/or specification. Also, key performance indicators as recommended by the World Bank Group ought to be such that is SMART compliant and cover the following performance areas:

- Delivery (obligated deliverables and outcomes)
- Support (contractual requirements)

- Quality (quality of products and services)
- Partnership and Innovation
- Governance and Risks (governance and compliance)
- Financial (financial information and documentation)

Part 2: Schedule of Works and Funds

Two documents namely, Program of Works and Cash Flow Projections constitute this part of the Contract Management Plan. Although the preparation of these two documents for the contract are not necessarily initiated by the project management team, instead by the contractor, the team reviews, approves and incorporate them into the Contract Management Plan.

Basically, the Program of Works reflects the start and end dates of basic and critical activities of the contract or the milestones of the implementation process as agreed with the service provider. The Cash Flow Projections is based on the Program of Works and the provisions of the contract. A typical Program of Works for a building construction contract and the Cash Flow Projection that considers monthly valuation and payment are shown in *Figure 9* and *Table 13* respectively.

Figure 9: Typical Program of Works *(Turn at 90°)*

S/N	Critical Task / Milestones	Period																			
		JAN, 21				FEB, 21				MAR, 21				APR, 21				JUN, 21			
		Wk1	Wk2	Wk3	Wk4	Wk1	Wk2	Wk3	Wk4	Wk1	Wk2	Wk3	Wk4	Wk1	Wk2	Wk3	Wk4	Wk1	Wk2	Wk3	Wk4
1	Mobilization																				
2	Substructure																				
3	Ground Floor Columns																				
4	Suspended Slab																				
5	1st Floor Columns																				
6	Roof Beams																				
7	Timber Carcassing																				
8	Roof Covering																				
	etc.																				

Table 13: Typical Cash Flow Projections

S/N	Month	Projected Gross Value of Works	Repayment of Advance Payment	Retention	Net Payment	Remarks
1	JAN, 31	30,000		1,500	28,500	
2	FEB, 28	20,000		1,000	19,000	
3	MAR, 31	35,000	4,000	1,750	29,250	
4	APR, 30	25,000	4,000	1,250	19,750	
5	MAY, 31	27,000	4,000	1,350	21,650	
6	JUN, 30	40,000		2,000	38,000	

Part 3: Roles and Responsibilities

Based on the nature and requirements of the contract, persons or entities that will be involved in management of the contract will have to be identified and each one's responsibilities resolved.

A good place to begin on the roles and responsibilities is to establish the contract organizational chart. A typical chart for a contract in a development agency supported program with an Implementation Unit (project management team) is shown in *Figure 10.*

Figure 10: Typical Contract Implementation Organogram

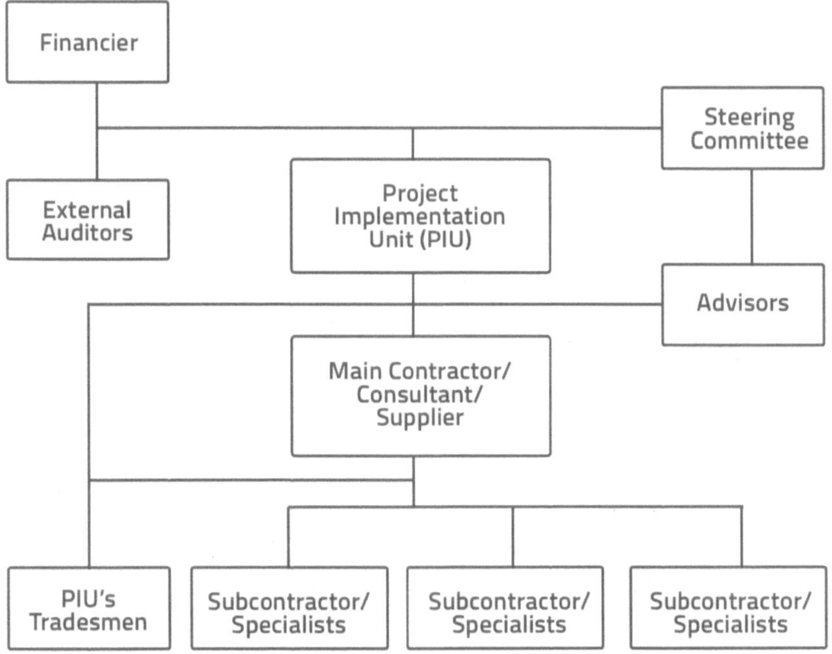

Without exhausting the list, some of the roles and responsibilities that are likely to be provided in a Contract Management Plan include:

- Financier
  - Review and Approval of Reports and Requests
  - Direct Payments
- Steering Committee
  - Formulation of guidelines and policies
  - Review and Approval or Reports and Requests
- Advisors
  - Technical Advice

  - Financial Advice
- Project Implementation Unit (Project Management Team)
  - Planning
  - Coordination
  - Cost Control
  - Instructions
  - Payment Requests
  - Procurement of Specialist/Nominated Sub-Contractors and Tradesmen
  - Controlling and monitoring of performance and compliance
  - Documentations and information management
  - Reporting
- Contractor/Supplier/Consultant
  - Planning
  - Work/supply/assignment execution
  - Assurance of quality and quantity of works, personnel and plant
  - Application for Payments
  - Insurance
  - Safety
  - Environmental protection
  - Security
  - Attendance to Nominated Sub-contractors/Suppliers and Tradesmen
  - Reporting
- Specialist/Nominated Sub-Contractors/Suppliers
  - Planning
  - Specialist works execution

- Direct Tradesmen
  - Planning
  - Trade/work execution
- Internal Auditors
  - Establishment/Examination of Internal Controls
  - Monitoring of Internal Controls
  - Reporting
- External Auditors
  - Financial Audits
  - Procurement Audits
  - Reporting
- External Performance Evaluation Team
  - Performance Review and Evaluation
  - Reporting
- Stakeholders
  - Environmental, social and economic impact assessment due to place, time and method/process of contract implementation
  - Reporting

Part 4: Communication and Reporting Procedures

This part of the Contract Management Plan provides Schedules that give details of:

- Mode of Communication
- Channel of Communication
- Anticipated Requests
- Anticipated Reports

Typical formats of these Schedules are shown in *Tables 14, 15, 16 and 17* overleaf.

Table 14: Schedule of Mode of Communication

Type of Communication	**Mode of Communication**
Invitations	Emails
Meetings	Minutes of Meeting
Requests	Letter via email
Approvals	Letter via email

Table 15: Schedule of Channel of Communication

<table>
<tr><th rowspan="2">Type of Communication</th><th colspan="2">Channel of Communication</th></tr>
<tr><td>From:</td><td>To:</td></tr>
<tr><td rowspan="2">Instructions to Contractor</td><td>Contract Manager</td><td>Contractor</td></tr>
<tr><td>Financier/Advisor/ MDAs</td><td>Contract Manager</td></tr>
<tr><td rowspan="2">Request for technical advice</td><td>Contractor</td><td>Contract Manager</td></tr>
<tr><td>Contract Manager</td><td>Advisor</td></tr>
<tr><td rowspan="2">Request for Payment</td><td>Contractor</td><td>Contract Manager</td></tr>
<tr><td>Contract Manager</td><td>Financier</td></tr>
</table>

Table 16: Schedule of Requests (Turn at 90°)

Request from	Type of Request	Request to	Receipt/ Endorsement by	Approval by	Action by
Contractor	Application for Payment	Owner	Advisor/ Contract Manager	MDA	Financier
	Application for Variation	Owner	Advisor/ Contract Manager	MDA	Financier
	Extension of Time	Owner	Advisor/ Contract Manager	MDA	Contract Manager
	Site Inspection	Contract Manager		Contract Manager	Advisor/ Contract Manager
Contract Manager	Reallocation of Funds	Financier	MDA	Financier	Contract Manager

Table 17: Schedule of Reports

Type of Report	**Report to**	**Frequency of reporting**
Progress Report	Contract Manager	Monthly
Soil Investigation	Contract Manager	One-off
Materials Inspection	Contract Manager	As required
Progress Report	MDA	Monthly
Progress Report	Steering Committee	Biennially
Audit Report	MDA	Annually

Part 5: Critical Contract Terms and Conditions

Although all the terms and conditions of the contract are very important, in planning for contract management purpose, some of them need to be classified as being critical since a slip on any of them is capable of frustrating or causing failure of the contract.

In a typical lump sum contract, such terms and conditions may relate to the issues highlighted in *Table 18*. This also constitutes the lists of relevant items the performance auditors expect the project management to have been paying attention to in the management of the contracts. "Particular Conditions of Contract" can provide a guide to these relevant items.

Table 18: Critical Contract Terms and Conditions

Relevant Term and Conditions	Brief Contract Information
Contract Price	• The contract price; • Key components of the price if necessary
Completion Period and Milestones	• Start Date and End Date of contract • Start Dates and End Dates of Milestones
Performance Security	• Nature of Instrument • Value and Currency • Expiring Date
Insurance	• Period for submission of evidence of insurance and relevant policies • Expiring Date for Insurance • Maximum amount of deductibles for insurance of Owner's risks • Minimum amount of third party insurance
Payments	• Advance Payment Amount • Advance Payment repayment amortization method • Intervals of Interim Payments • Minimum amount of Interim Payment Certificate • Period of honoring Payment Certificates • Interest on unpaid certified payment • Percentage of Retention • Limit amount of Retention
Variations	• Approving authorities' thresholds for variation of contract price • Method of pricing variations

Relevant Term and Conditions	Brief Contract Information
Price Adjustments (Fluctuations)	• Method of computations for price fluctuation
Claims	• Period between potential claim event and initiation of claim • Period of response to claims
Provisional Sums	• Items of Provisional Sums • Procurement method for award of sub-contracts • Percentage for adjustment of Provisional Sums
Extension of Time	• Basic conditions for extension of time • Procedures for extension of time
Suspension of Work	• Basic conditions for extension of time • Procedures for extension of time
Dispute Resolution	• Method of dispute resolution • Stages/Levels of dispute resolution
Termination of Contract	• Key conditions for Owners termination of contract • Key conditions for Contractor's termination of contract • Basic procedures with timelines for termination of contract

Part 6: Risks and Mitigation

The identification and mitigation of risks are essential elements of contract management and therefore need included as part of the plan abnitio.

An understanding of what is 'risk' is required to carry out this exercise. According to UK Association of Project Management (APM, 2019), *risk is an uncertain event or set of circumstances that, should it occur, will have an effect on the achievement of the project's objectives.*

The attempt at this stage to provide solutions for a minimized impact of these uncertain events should they occur sets the tone for actual risk management during the contract. For its projects, the World Bank has identified some generic risks that the project management team of the projects may consider to include in their risk management plan to guarantee effective management of the project's contracts. These risks are:

- Lack of upfront setting of contract management requirements;
- Little or no enforcement of contract deliverables, resulting in payments not appropriately controlled or managed;
- No concluding contractual review, so actual results are not clear;
- Poor contract reporting and communication process leads to confusion, poor performance and missed opportunities;
- Poor contract management meetings lead to conflict, misunderstanding, and bad results;
- Poor senior management control reinforces poor contract management practice on the ground.

Notwithstanding the above, every contract has its peculiarity of risks though in most cases, they all border on these five endogenous uncertainties which are fundamentally important to contract performance (**Chapman and Ward, 2011**):

- Variability associated with estimates

- Uncertainties about the basis of estimates
- Uncertainties about design and logistics
- Uncertainties about objectives and priorities
- Uncertainty about fundamental relationships between project parties.

It is around these uncertainties that one can generate potential risks peculiar to the contract. Most importantly here are the risks arising from the relationships between project parties which most time are due to ambiguity in respect of:

- Specification of responsibilities
- Perceptions of roles and responsibilities
- Communication across interfaces
- The capability of parties
- Formal contractual conditions and their effects
- Informal understanding on top of, or instead of, formal contracts
- Mechanisms for co-ordination and control.

(Chapman and Ward, 2003)

One other uncertainty that may also constrain performance and therefore must not be forgotten is the behavior of the external approving authorities. The turnaround response, for example, from these authorities is significant risks that have to be recognized and properly accommodated.

In totality, this part of the Contract Management Plan typical of *Table 19* consists of the Risk Management Plan produced at this stage.

Table 19: Typical Risks Management Plan Structure
(Turn at 90°)

S/N	Risk	Risk Sources	Anticipated Occurrence Point on PLC[1]	Assigned Risk Level[2]	Mitigation		
					Action	Person/ Entity Responsible	Monitoring and Controls by:

[1] – Project Life Cycle

[2] – High Risk; Moderate Risk; Low Risk

Part 7: Contract Management Performance Framework and Measurement

This part of the Contract Management Plan set the pace for measuring the management performance of the contract from the perspectives of the different members of the contract management team including the project management team. According to Peter Drucker, "you can't manage what you can't measure" **(Drucker, 1973)**. In order words, part of developing contract management plan is to first have the success of the contract management performance defined in terms of SMART activities associated with the contract. SMART is "specific, measurable, achievable, relevant and time bound". In this way, neither the project management team nor the performance auditor gets lost at any time of what is expected in determining the extent of success of the contract management.

One technique that can be employed in developing the framework for measurement and evaluation of the contract management performance is Balanced Scorecard.

Balanced Scorecard

This is a management tool that provides stakeholders with a comprehensive measure of how the team is progressing towards the achievement of its strategic goal.

Whilst principally, for most development agencies' supported projects, the stakeholders are the Financier, Steering Committee, Other Approving Authorities, Project Implementation Unit (project management team) and the Contractor/Supplier/Consultant, the strategic goal of contract management as always is to have the contractual deliverables delivered in the right quantity and quality, at the right time and right cost. Balanced Scorecard identifies endogenously within the contract management team, factors and activities in a mapping order that drives effective and efficient contract management and creates utmost contract performance value.

A typical strategic contract management map for works contract is shown *Figure 11* overleaf.

Figure 11: Strategic Contract Management Mapping
(Turn at 90°)

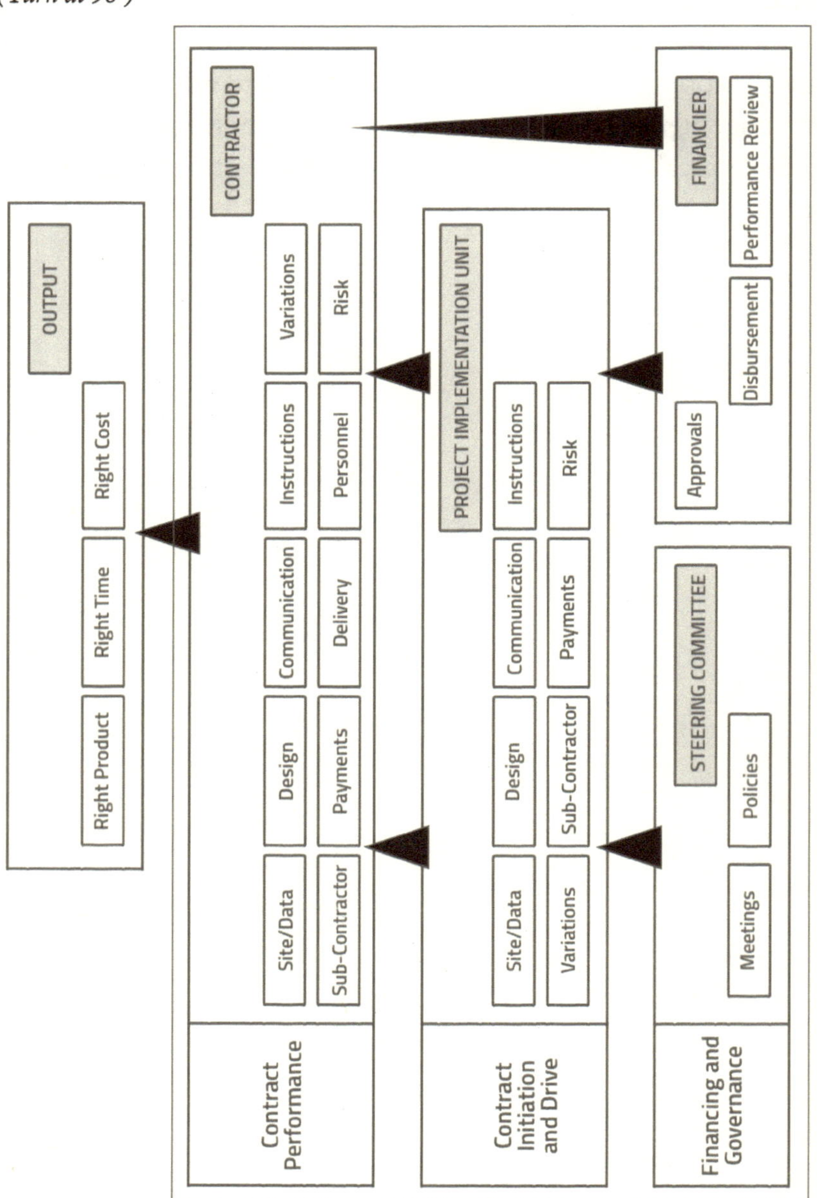

Based on the above mapping showing key performance areas for the different units of the contract management team, the SMART activities for each of the units have been identified and collectively form the management Balanced Scorecard towards utmost contract performance. The Balanced Scorecard as typified in *Tables 20, 21, 22 and 23* is the framework upon which each unit (Contractor, Project Management Team, Steering Committee, Financier) and jointly the team at large will be evaluated.

Table 20: Scorecard: Contractor (*Turn at 90°*)

Key Performance Area	Performance Contribution	Key Performance Indicator
Site/Data/ Information	Site Mobilization, receipt of relevant information and presentation of preliminary essential documents.	• Period of effective mobilization to site; • Period of presentation of Advance Payment Guarantee; • Period of presentation of Performance Security; • Period of presentation of insurance policy; • Period of reconfirmation and presentation of Work Program • Period of collection of initial data and/or information; • Period of request for clarifications on initial data and/or information
Design/Contract Requirement	Completeness of design/ requirements and production of workshop drawings	• Time taken to make initial request for clarification and/or completion of design/contract requirements; • Average time between request for elemental design/ requirement details and expected date of implementation; • Average time between date of submission of workshop drawings and expected date of implementation.

Key Performance Area	Performance Contribution	Key Performance Indicator
Communication	Use of mode and channel of approved channel of communication; provision of reports and response to requests	• Number of times specified mode of communication is not used; • Number of times specified channel of communication is not used; • Number of requests received; • Number of requests responded to; • Average time taken to respond to requests • Timely preparation and circulation of reports.
Instructions	Response to contractual instructions	• Number of oral instructions received; • Average time taken to request for confirmation of oral instructions; • Average time between date of receipt of instruction and date of request for clarifications; • Number of instructions not complied to; • Average time lag between date of receiving instruction and compliance on the expected date;

Key Performance Area	Performance Contribution	Key Performance Indicator
Variations	Changes to contract ordered.	• Average time taken to provide advice on cost and time impact of variation upon receipt of proposal for variation; • Divergence of the variation item rates from the contract rates
Sub-contractors and Tradesmen	Engagement of Sub-contractors and Tradesmen	• Period between the date Contractor requests for engagement of Sub-contractors/Tradesmen and expected start date of implementation of the specialist works; • Average period of receiving Performance Security and Advance Payment Guarantee from Sub-contractors; • Period between the date of being prepared to receive Sub-contractors/Tradesmen (i.e providing attendance) and expected start date of implementation of the specialist works; • Level and quality of the attendance provided to Sub-contractors/Tradesmen; • Period between receipt of Sub-contractor's application for payment and date of submission of same to Client; • Period between receipt of Sub-contractor's moneys and date of transfer of payment to them;

Key Performance Area	Performance Contribution	Key Performance Indicator
Payments	Payments	• Regularity of request/application for valuation and certification; • Regularity of achieving threshold value qualification for payment on appointed dates of valuation; • Margin of adherence to milestone performance to necessitate milestones payments (variance between due date and performance date).
Delivery	Time, quality and quantity of deliverable.	• Number of times work items in the work plan are not met; • Number of times work plan is revised; • Number of times extension of time not due to variation is requested; • Margin of deviation from completion date; • Number of times quality of performance is rejected; • Number of times deviation from contract specification occurs; • Magnitude of shortfall in the quantity of deliverables.

Key Performance Area	Performance Contribution	Key Performance Indicator
Personnel	Number, capacity and availability of personnel	• Number of personnel; • Number of qualified personnel; • Deviations of available qualified personnel from the contractual number; • Number of personnel rejected due to poor quality performance; • Rate of turnover of qualified personnel engaged on the contract.
Financials	Financial issues relating to price fluctuation.	• Purchases of materials for which advance payment is received; • Period between receipt of advance payment and placement of order for specified materials; • Number of times request for fluctuation claims are made; • Completeness of the details of daywork records

Key Performance Area	Performance Contribution	Key Performance Indicator
Risks	Mitigation of Risks	• Maintenance of insurance policies (number of times premium is not paid) • Average period between date of expiration of one insurance policy and date of start of another; • Number of times insurance policies are rejected due to inappropriate value; • Average period between date of expiration of one performance security and date of start of another; • Number of times performance security is rejected due to inappropriate value; • Level of mitigation of all identified risks

Table 21: Scorecard: Project Implementation Unit (Project Management Team) (Turn at 90°)

Key Performance Area	Performance Contribution	Key Performance Indicator
Site/Data/ Information	Handing over of sites and provision of relevant information to the Contractor	• Time taken to handover site; • Time taken to supply initial data and/or information; • Sufficiency of initial data and/or information
Design	Readiness and completeness of design/requirements	• Overall completeness of design at start date; • Number of work elements with no design; • Number of work elements with incomplete design; • Average time between date of making available complete designs and the date they are required; • Average time taken to approve workshop drawings.
Communication	Use of mode and channel of approved channel of communication; provision of reports and response to requests	• Number of times specified mode of communication is not used; • Number of times specified channel of communication is not used; • Number of requests received; • Number of requests responded to; • Average time taken to respond to requests • Timely preparation and circulation of reports.

Key Performance Area	Performance Contribution	Key Performance Indicator
Instructions	Issuance of contractual instructions	• Number of oral instructions issued; • Average time taken to confirm oral instructions; • Average time lag between date of instruction and expected date of required action; • Clarity of instructions (Number of instructions issued that clarification is sought).
Variations	Changes to contract ordered.	• Number of changes to the contract ordered; • Net value of changes to the contract ordered; • Net addition to completion period due to changes to the contract ordered.
Sub-contractors and Tradesmen	Engagement of Sub-contractors and Tradesmen	• Period of employment process of nominated sub-contractors; • Period between the date of employment of sub-contractor and expected start date of implementation of sub-contract work; • Period between the date of employment of Tradesmen and expected start date of implementation of tradesmen work

Key Performance Area	Performance Contribution	Key Performance Indicator
Payments	Payments	• Regularity of valuation and certification; • Average time between valuation and certification dates; • Average period of honoring certificate; • Adherence to milestones payments (variance between due date and payment date).
Risks	Management of Risks	• Level of mitigation of identified risks

Table 22: Scorecard: Steering Committee (*Turn at 90°*)

Key Performance Area	Performance Contribution	Key Performance Indicator
Meetings	Meetings to review reports, provide guidelines and develop policies towards the contract.	• Number of meetings held; • Difference between number of meetings held and the required number; • Number of periods the required number of meetings was not met; • Number of meetings with full attendance of the members; • Average participation of members at meetings; • Number of requested emergency meetings that took place; • Number of requested emergency meetings that failed to take place.
Policies, guidelines and instructions	Development of policies and guidelines and issuance of necessary instructions	• Number of contract management related policies and guidelines developed or affirmed; • Period between date of a request for guidance and the date one was provided; • Period between date of a request for approval and the date of response.

Table 23: Scorecard: Financier (*Turn at 90°*)

Key Performance Area	Performance Contribution	Key Performance Indicator
Approval and Document Reviews		• Average time taken to carry out reviews of requests and grant no-objections.
Disbursements		• Average period between date of request for payment and actual disbursement; • Average turn around period seeking clarification upon receiving payment application.
Performance Review		• Number of visits to site; • Number of feedbacks issued; • Time taken to issue feedback.

Implementation of the Contract Management Plan

The primary evidence of an attempt by the project management team to exercise effective contract management of the contracts under the project is the existence of a Contract Management Plan for each of the contracts. The performance auditor will strongly desire to see this. Where Contract Management Plan exists, it serves as an instrument of guidance, control, monitoring and evaluation of the performance of the contract. Indeed, for the performance auditor, the content and implementation of this document fully form the basis of the assessment of the performance of the contracts and by extension, significantly, the project.

More than the project management team just having the Contract Management Plan, the performance auditor will like to see how the implementation of the plan has progressed. The auditor will examine how actions over the period have matched with plan. On the part of the project management team, its confidence in being spotless in the management of the contract indeed in no other better way starts with the development of Contract Management Plan. All things being equal, if the project management team had determined to and indeed followed the plan as expounded above, excellent result worthy of commendation by the performance auditor will be realized.

The attitude of the team should be to keep an eye on the contract deliverables and time, and adopt the right principles towards the contract management. These principles must include:

- **Accountability**

Everyone must know what his role is in the contract and

acknowledge specific events, activities or tasks of which the performance or failure are exclusively linked to his actions or inaction at specific time.

There must be this understanding that there is no identifiable event, activity or task that is no one's or severally everyone's responsibility.

- **Transparency**

Openness is character that must be seen in everyone's actions. Openness include that all contract documents (drawings, specifications, terms of reference, agreement, conditions of contract, etc) are explicit to everyone's understanding.

The intentions and meanings of documents, information and communication exchanged at all times must be one and the same - no ambiguity or hidden agenda.

And where the onus lies on one to understand and act, he should seek clarity if need be and not depend on wrong or mischievous assumptions.

- **Integrity**

Demonstration of integrity is that one does what is required of him to do at the right time to which he has earlier said or agreed to do.

There must be a deliberate resolve that words, plans and obligations are duly honored.

Moreover, under no circumstance should one in doing what he ought to do take undue advantage or seek unwarranted rewards.

- **Commitment**

This entails strong expression of willingness to act and indeed do all things reasonably possible so as to act, removing all anticipated constraints and ultimately act.

In the context of contract management, "I will try" or "I will do my best" are not acceptable. The norm regarding obligations, expectations and promises should be "I will" except the conditions fundamentally change and an understanding is reached with the relevant stakeholder.

Commitment is not only heard but also seen.

CASH FLOW MANAGEMENT

Having established the Work Plan and the Budget, cash flow management relates not only to the financing of the budget but also to the very important matter of where, how, how much, and when fund inflows are received and expenditure outflows are made on the implementation of the project. The primary essence of cash flow management is to ensure that neither insufficient nor unreasonably excess cash is available per time to meet the expected activities of the project as per the Work Plan and Budget. This is fundamental to the performance of the project. Non availability of cash particularly when it is needed can lead to delays, frustration or even abandonment of the project. In an environment where inflation, unfavourable exchange rate and interest rate are prevalent, the cost of executing delayed activities becomes higher than that had the funds been available at the right time. Where also there are much fund available at a time than required and necessary, not only will misuse likely to result and opportunity cost of holding idle funds incurred, cost of financing is increased as funds are withdrawn earlier than anticipated; all of these add to the overall cost of the project and lead to cost overrun. The purpose of cash flow management is to neutralize the low or high cash situation in the project.

Focus of the Performance Auditor

With all the dangers of inappropriate cash flow in the project, it is obvious what the performance auditor would be looking out with respect to cash flows when examining the performance of the project. The first reference point is the Work Plan and Budget. The second is the plan for the financing of the budget. This plan should provide information on the sources of funds for the project and the schedule of the receipts of the funds in specified amounts and dates.

There are two levels of assessment the performance auditor will focus on to make judgment on the cash flow management in the project. The first is the extent of reasonability in the cash flow plan. He will want to see that there is strong match between when amounts of funds are planned to be received in a given period, with the level/cost of activities scheduled for the same period. If the difference between the Budgeted Cost of Work Schedule (BCWS) and the Planned Inflow (PIN) does not tend to zero in almost all the periods, the project is already planned to have liquidity problem. The framework of the comparison between BCWS and PIN is shown in *Table 24*.

Table 24: Comparison of Budgeted Cost of Work Schedule and Planned Fund Inflow

Period	WBS Element	BCWS	Planned Inflow (PIN)	BCWS – PIN	Sources of Inflow
Year 1: Quarter 1	a. Substructure b. Framework	$7,500	$6,800	$700	
Year 1: Quarter 2	c. Roof structure	$3,500	$4,000	($500)	
Year 1: Quarter 3	d. Finishings	$11,000	$11,200	($200)	

The second level of assessment is critical to the auditor's opinion on the cash flow management. The opinion is based on the interpretation of the outcome of the analysis of the cash flow management as observed during the period under review. The structure of the analysis is typified in *Table 25*. The parameters for the analysis include BCWS, ACWP, PIN and Actual Inflow (AIN).

Table 25: Analysis of the Cash Flow Management

(1) Period	(2) WBS Element	(3) BCWS	(4) ACWP	(5) Planned Inflow (PIN)	(6) Actual Inflow (AIN)	(7) BCWS – AIN	(8) ACWP - AIN	(9) PIN – AIN
Year 1: Quarter 1								
Year 1: Quarter 2								
Year 1: Quarter 3								
Year 1: Quarter 4								

Some of the deductions that the performance auditor may make based on the results of columns 7, 8, and 9 of *Table 25* in a given period include:

Column 7:

- If BCWS > AIN, then among other issues, may be:
  - The work is slow;
  - The budget variance is favourable;
  - The funds are not coming in as expected for the works.

- If BCWS < AIN, then among other issues, may be:
  - The budget variance is favourable;
  - The project is operating with excess cash.

Column 8:

- If ACWP > AIN, then among other issues, may be:
  - The budget variance is adverse;
  - The project is operating with cash deficit;
  - The debt profile of the project is on the increase;

- If ACWP < AIN, then among other issues, may be:
  - The budget variance is favourable;
  - The project is operating with excess cash;

Column 9:

- If PIN > AIN, then among other issues, may be:
  - The work is slow;
  - The project is operating with cash deficit;
  - The debt profile of the project is on the increase;

- If PIN < AIN, then among other issues, may be:
  - The budget variance is favourable;
  - The project is operating with excess cash;

Preparation of Cash Flow Plan

As always, there are two sides of the Cash Flow Plan namely the inflows and outflows. The outflows are the expenditures made under and/or on behalf of the project. The inflows are the funds coming into the project or made on behalf of the project to finance the project activities. Generally, in projects, these inflows may come from multiple sources in different amounts. But in development agencies' supported projects, the inflows are predominantly from an agency or syndicate agencies as the case may be. The other portion of inflow may be the counterpart funding from the loan/grant recipient or implementing agency.

What is critical in preparing Cash Flow Plan in such projects is understanding how funds are released from the financing agency(ies). The 'how' here includes requirements and process of application by the project for release of funds, expected time lag between time of receiving the application and the actual release of funds, fund release thresholds per time, and the currency and exchange rate conversion mechanism of the funds to be released in a given occasion. For most development agencies, this information is contained in their Disbursement Manual. The disbursement manual spells out the disbursement methods that are also stipulated in the financing agreement or other related documents such as disbursement letter. Without full grasp of these disbursement methods, one cannot prepare effective Cash Flow Plan.

Disbursement Methods

For most development agencies, there are basically four disbursement methods applicable in their projects. These are:

i. Reimbursement;
ii. Advance;
iii. Direct Payment; and
iv. Reimbursement Guarantee.

Reimbursement

Reimbursement method involves the development agency reimburse the project the value of expenditures made on the project in respect of the executed portion of the project that the agency is due to finance under the financing agreement.

That is, the part that has been prefinanced by the project is reimbursed to it by the development agency.

However, this reimbursement is predicated on the condition that the expenditures are eligible. It is also not expected that this prefinanced portion constitutes very large part of the project by value. Additionally, in requesting for the reimbursement, there must be evidence of the payment covering amount paid, the date and the payee; all reflected in the Interim Financial Report or Statement of Expenditure.

Because of these much requirements, this method of disbursement is very difficult for the project to enjoy and thus a bit unreliable in supporting the cash flow of the project.

Advance

This is a system where the development agency advances funds to the project in a designated account known as Special Account for the purpose of financing expenditures the project is to incur in the near future in the implementation of the project. Such expenditures as required are mostly recurrent project expenditure, small works and goods. This account is usually replenished by the development agency upon request by the project as the balance falls to a predetermined limit. For most development agency, the request, balance limits and the replenishment are conditioned on the following:

i. That the request covers anticipated expenditures for the next six months based on the project's budget;
ii. The advance received before the last one was made have been fully utilized by the project;
iii. The older advances including 50% of the one before the last have been justified by the project;

iv. The replenishment will not cause the balance in the account to exceed a predetermined ceiling;
v. No advance is made after the disbursement deadline date;
vi. Balance in the account after closing date of the project shall be refunded shortly after the date except if expanded eligible expenditures have been agreed.

Direct Payment

Direct payment involves the disbursement of funds by the development agency directly to a third party (beneficiary) upon the request of the project for payments in respect of works, goods or services provided to the project. This third party - the beneficiary of the payment may be contractors, suppliers or consultants employed under the project.

The request for direct payment is usually honoured so long as there is a proof of valid contract between the project and the third party and the activity for which the payment is being requested for is eligible and had been certified by the project. This disbursement method is a bit easier in letting in funds into the project and less time consuming. However, the frequency of use may be constrained by the minimum threshold that the development agency allows for a single request.

Reimbursement Guarantee

This is where the development agency makes a special commitment that is irrevocable to reimburse a commercial bank for payment it has made to a third party against a Letter of Credit issued in respect of expenditures on the project. The use of this method of payment is peculiar to transactions on imported goods for the project. The process of application of the method can be briefly described as follows:

i. Contract is awarded by the project to a Supplier located abroad to supply (export) goods to the project;

iv. ii. The Supplier causes the project to obtain from a local Bank a Letter of Credit (LC) which is primarily an undertaken that the Bank will pay the Supplier if the project fails to pay the Supplier within a stated credit period;

v. iii. The local Bank (issuing Bank) sends the LC to its correspondence Bank located in the same place as the Supplier. This correspondence Bank which may be both advising and confirming Bank undertakes to make the payment to the Supplier upon confirmation that the goods have been shipped to the project;

vi. iv. The project presents to the development agency a copy of the LC and a request to it to make commitment through its issuance of Reimbursement Guarantee to reimburse the confirming Bank whenever the Bank forwards its claim in respect of payment made to the Supplier for the goods shipped or delivered to the project.

Figure 12 illustrates this process with encircled numbers indicating the sequence of the steps.

Figure 12: The workings of Letter of Credit and Reimbursement Guarantee

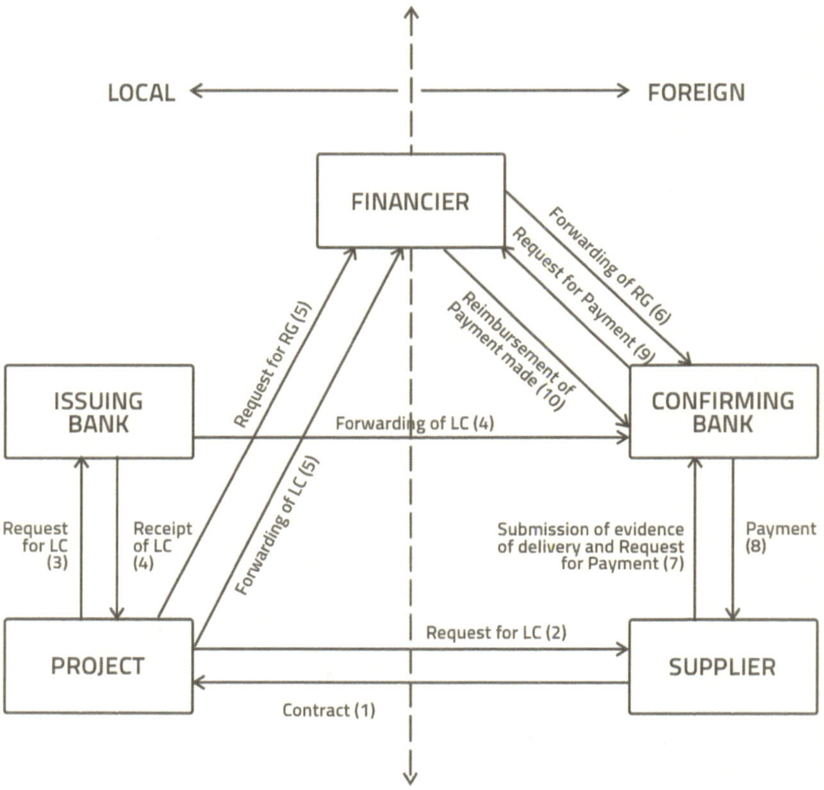

This process can be cumbersome and time consuming particularly where the reputation of the project, the local Bank and the country is not good in the eyes of the Supplier and the confirming Bank. But when once the process is gotten to the point of the development agency making the special commitment and the confirming Bank accepting same, the inflow through this method becomes smooth and fast.

With a clear understanding of the conditions associated with the different disbursement methods as outlined above, the Disbursement Plan can be successfully developed as such to contribute to effective and efficient cash flow in the project.

Management of the Cash Flow

Management of cash flow in the development agencies' project is primarily anchored on the management of the disbursement flow and activities implementation. When careful attention is paid and actions taken towards both simultaneously, effective and efficient cash flow management can be achieved. All things being equal, to balance the activities implementation, the disbursement flow must be right. This is why as efforts are made on procurement and contract managements, getting smooth approvals for request, and engagement of non-financial resources - all to drive activities implementation, the concentration for cash flow management should be more on the disbursement flow.

Disbursements and Fund Flows

Understanding of the conditions associated with the different disbursement methods outlined above is essential to cash flow management. All of these impact on the actual inflow to the project with regards to advances, direct payment or reimbursements from the financier and therefore must be factored into the cash flow planning and management. The time lag between the request date and actual replenishment of the special account, or direct payment or reimbursement to third party require special consideration in the cash flow management. This time lag depends on the quality of the requests, turn-around time in response to the requests, and the fund flow mechanism in place.

The quality of the requests entails that all the requirements are adhered to and the demanded accompanying document submitted, giving no opportunity to the development agency to continue to seek for clarifications or turn down the request. Some of these documents which the capacity to prepare should reside in the project are shown in *Table 26* for the different disbursement methods. The preparation and submission of these documents are critical as any shortfall in the completeness of any may cause delay in its passage or lead to rejection of the request – all of which adversely will affect the project's cash flow. Other factors that may affect the disbursement flow and must be avoided are the inclusion of ineligible expenditures in any of the documents at any time or incorrectness of the account to which payment is advised to be made.

Additionally, in order to avert the adverse impact of delayed disbursement flow, it is important that in managing the cash flow, the project management team have an idea of the average turn-around time in response to requests made to the development agency. This can be known from the project documents and experience and planned for.

Finally, the set fund flow for the project should be properly considered. Fund flow relates to the tiers involved in the flow of the funds from the financiers to finally the recipient of the funds under the project. The larger the number of tiers, most likely the more time it would take to have effective payment for project expenditures. This has to be factored in in the cash flow management for the project.

Table 26: Accompanying Documents to Request for Disbursements (Turn at 90°)

S/N	Disbursement Method	Mandatory Document		Additional Document
1.	Reimbursement	**a.**	Formal letter signed by authorized signatures requesting for a specific amount to be paid into a specified account in respect of eligible items of the project that expenditures have not been made on previously.	Copy of the Contract/ Purchase Order/ Invoice in respect of the expenditure; Interim or Completion Certificate; Receipt Notes and Acceptance Certificate
		b.	Statement of Expenditures made on eligible items indicating to whom the payment was made to; the purpose of the payment; total commitment regarding an expenditure that a portion or complete payment has been made; date of the payment; mode of payment - cheque or cash; and evidence of payment – receipts or bank transaction advice.	

S/N	Disbursement Method	Mandatory Document		Additional Document
		c.	Summary of program and estimated budget of activities covering a period of six months obtained from a previously approved Work Program. This summary contains the description, quantity, country of origin and estimated cost of the goods/services and the respective amount being currently requested for disbursement.	
2.	Advance	**a.**	As in Item 1(a) above.	As in Items 1(i) – (iii) above.
		b.	As in Item 1(b) above.	
		c.	As in Item 1(c) above.	
		d.	Special Account Reconciliation	
		e.	Bank Statement of Special Account	

S/N	Disbursement Method	Mandatory Document		Additional Document
3.	Direct Payment	**a.**	As in Item 1(a) above.	
		b.	As in Item 1(b) above.	
		c.	Copy of the Contract/Purchase Order	
		d.	Invoice	
		e.	Interim or Completion Certificate	
		f.	Delivery Note and Acceptance Certificate	
4.	Reimbursement Guarantee	**a.**	Formal letter signed by authorized signatures requesting for a Reimbursement Guarantee in a particular amount and to beneficiary in connection with an issued Letter of Credit.	
		b.	Copy of valid Letter of Credit	
		c.	Copy of the Contract/Purchase Order	

CHAPTER FOUR

FIDUCIARY AUDIT

In the course of the examination of the performance, the financial state, and the progress of projects financed by the development agencies, one area that the reviewers always pay attention to is the extent of compliance on the part of the project management team with the fiduciary requirements associated with the project. It is therefore important that the team and the project implementation agency indeed understand these fiduciary requirements.

Meaning of Fiduciary

According to Wikipedia (https://en.wikipedia.org/wiki/Fiduciary), "a **fiduciary** is a person who holds a legal or ethical relationship of trust with one or more other parties (person or group of persons)" The legal or ethical relationship of trust typically relates to one taking care of the other's money or other assets. Fiduciary duty or responsibility arise on the part of one (an entity) when due to confidence and trust reposed on him (the entity) by a person (another entity) undertakes to in a prudent manner in a particular matter such as management of funds acts on behalf of that person (other entity) with best interest of that person (the other entity) upheld in all aspects.

In the context of development agencies' funded projects, of

the resources (funds, tangible and intangible assets) released by the development agency, the recipient cum the project management team and project implementation agency undertake to use them exclusively for the intended purposes with strong consideration for economy, efficiency and social benefits. Accepting the resources from the development agency places a duty on the part of the recipient to exercise prudence, use the funds for the established purposes, safeguard the resources, act in the best interest of the agency, and conduct its affairs such that it is not seen to be failing in these responsibilities.

In order not to live this duty to chance, the development agency in every of its projects provides policies and guidelines of which if the recipients or the project management team follow along with the provisions of the financing agreement will by default be responsive to these expected duties. In other words, a measure of observation of the financing agreement, policies and guidelines to fulfill this duty on the part of the project management team is a measure of the fiduciary compliance. The significance of fiduciary compliance is the assurance of the safeguard of the resources against all kinds of risks. In addition, it is that the purpose for which the resources were made available is effectively pursued by the recipients or its agents and not deviated from.

Focus of Fiduciary Compliance Assessment

Usually, the focus of the fiduciary compliance assessment is on the control risk areas of the project management. These risk areas among others include predominantly the financial management. In a more general term, the assessment will touch on the project management team's disposition towards the followings:

- Financing Agreement;
- Financial Management:
    - Project Management Team Capacity;
    - Fund Flow;
    - Work Planning and Budget;
    - Internal Control;
    - Accounting and Financial Reporting;
    - Internal Audit;
    - External Audit;
    - Disbursement; and
    - Counterpart Fund
- Procurement and Contract Management;
- Project Management Reports;
- Records Management; and
- Anti-Corruption

Most of these areas have been covered in different parts of the book with respect to what the project management team should know concerning them and the specific preparation required of the team to satisfy the auditor and earn his commendations. However, it will still be good under this Chapter to mention exactly what the reviewers will be looking for, and why, and some of the indicators that ascertain the level of compliance with fiduciary requirements.

Financing Agreement

The Financing Agreement is a top priority document for the project as it contains the legal covenants expected of the implementing agency and/or the project management team to fulfill. Sometimes, there are some conditions in the agreement that must be fulfilled within a specified period in order to confer effectiveness to the agreement. The ease and the speed of the fulfillment of these conditions to a reasonable extent indicate the preparedness of the project management team to implement the project as agreed. Some of such conditions needing to be satisfied early may include establishment of Project Implementation Unit and project governance structure, opening of Special Account, guarantee of the source of counterpart fund, etc.

Other terms of the agreement may require that certain documents are submitted to the financiers at specified dates during the implementation of the project, for instance, Interim Unaudited Financial Reports, Progress Reports, Annual Budget, etc. The reviewer will check the observation of these submission dates.

The intention of the terms and conditions constituting legal covenants provided in the agreement is to guarantee the success of the project in achieving its development objectives and therefore cannot be ignored.

Financial Management

This is the major constituent of fiducial responsibility in view that good financial management is essential for the assurance of and actual realization of the project. According to the World Bank, excellent financial management entails that:

- relevant project information needed by those who manage, implement, supervise and exercise oversight functions are provided;

- there exists an assurance that the funds are being utilized both efficiently and for the purposes intended; and
- opportunities for fraud and corruption are minimized and the attempt easily forestalled or detected.

In these regards, therefore, assessment of the financial management will, relative to best practices, and in accordance with the financing agreement consider the operations of or activities of the project management team in the following aspects of the project management:

- Team Capacity;
- Fund Flow;
- Work Planning and Budget;
- Internal Control;
- Accounting and Financial Reporting;
- Internal Audit;
- External Audit;
- Disbursement; and
- Counterpart Fund

Project Management Team Capacity

The capacity of the project management team is critical to successful financial management. First and foremost, the composition of the team should be such that there is a complete representation of the professionals required for the different aspects of financial management. These may include in good number accountants, finance experts, project management experts, and depending on the nature of the project, quantity surveyors, contract managers, engineers, etc. It is expected that more than anything else, these team members should have relevant educational and professional qualifications, and reasonable experience. To the reviewer, sound financial management is most assured when these qualities are observed of the project management team.

Fund Flow

Fund flow relates to the tiers involved in and the smoothness of flow of the funds from the financiers (including the counterpart funds) to finally the recipient or beneficiary of the funds under the project. The more complex the structure of the fund flow and number of tiers are, the less smooth and slower it is to have effective payment for project expenditures. With a higher number of tiers, the probability of distortion in the flow and the consequential ripple effect leading to irregularity and delay in payment is much higher. Therefore, knowing the enormous adverse impact delays in payment can have on the project which includes extension of completion period and cost overrun, the reviewer will focus the assessment on the complexity and tiers of the fund flow.

Work Plan and Budget

Work Plan and Budget are among the documents most financing agreement will require the project management team to after due approval by the project steering committee submit to the financing development agency annually within a specified period prior to the beginning of the year the plan covers. The process of both the project governance and development agencies' approvals of these document at the right times and regularity of the submissions would be the first check on the Work Plan and Budget.

The preparation of the Work Plan and Budget is another consideration. The level of participation of the officers and entities connected to the project and rightfully supposed to be involved in the preparation is key here and would be assessed. This also leads to the matter of the comprehensiveness and cost estimates of the Work Plan and Budget. When the Work Plan do not capture all the tasks of the project for the period or the costs are not reasonably estimated, it may lead to ill performance or disruption of cash flows or cost overrun or even frustration of the project.

Another and most important aspect of the review is the assessment of the periodic performance of the Work Plan, Budget, and Budget vis-à-vis the Work Plan. These involve comparing the planned with the actuals. Lack of match between the actual work performed (or expenditure) and work schedule (actual is less than planned) may indicate:

- lack of planning capacity, or
- lack of capacity to implement the plan, or
- over ambition, or
- approval process constraints.

Where upon variance analysis of the periodic Budgets, it turns out that for most periods, the expenditures are significantly below the budget, all of the above could also be deduced. Where the expenditure is much higher, probably there is weak or absence of cost control.

Furthermore, the assessment of Work Plan and Budget will include a check if there exist system of tracking budget estimates and expenses and linking same to output from the work schedule for a given period. Finally, the reviewer will like to see Budget Reports produced by the project management team at the end of each budget period. Having this report will first show the commitment of the team to review its performance and willingness to take corrective measures to improve performance.

Internal Control

Internal control is considered active when there exist a process that guarantees reliability of financial reporting, effectiveness and efficiency of operations and compliance with good practice and laws **(PCAOB, n.d.)**. The first test of internal control is the existence of developed policies and procedures aimed at creating control environment and system for monitoring financial activities. Where this document exists, it will along with best practices form the basis of the assessment of the internal control. Some of the areas expected to be provided in this document which the reviewer will observe the implementation include:

- authorization procedures;
- measures of safeguarding the assets;
- accounting procedures;
- payment processes; and
- procurement processes.

Though not intended as a staff audit, among the key elements of the internal control review is the examination of the staffing of the project including the project governance with respect to:

- qualifications;
- functions; and

- levels of authority and responsibility.

The aim of this examination is to ensure that there is appropriate segregation of duties and a good match between qualification and responsibility.

As part of cash management which is critical in both safeguarding moneys and being prudent, internal control assessment will also involve a check on:

- The limit of cash transaction taking place in the project implementation unit to ensure that it is not unreasonably high;
- The reconciliation of bank balances to ensure that it is conducted monthly and timely; and
- Contract commitments to ensure that funds are available at the right time for the financing.

Accounting and Financial Reporting

Accounting of the funds received and expenditure made is among the primary factors of financial management. Accounting involves recording movement of funds and transactions and the reporting of same. The key assessment here is the tools employed and the manner in which the recording and reporting are done by the project management team. The tools may include manual or computerized accounting system. Where computerized, the rating of the accounting and financial reporting by the reviewer would be high particularly if the software in use covers all books of accounts and is online based as such all the accounts are updated in real time with all transaction postings. For such accounting system, the expectation of timely recording of transactions and financial reporting are achieved as all the relevant financial statements can be generated in good time to meet the demands of the users including the auditors and development agencies.

The target is to see that the project management team has on demand or at the times specified in the financial agreement and/ or other financial guidelines the information on the financial state of the project through its books of accounts ranging from General Ledger, Cash book, Personnel Information System, Fixed Asset Register, Contract Accounting, etc. presented in the prescribed accounting standard.

Internal Audit

Audit will reveal the strength of the internal control in place and provide the opportunity for corrective measures. Whether or how this goal is being achieved would be the subject of the internal audit's examination. According to Institute of Internal Auditors, "internal auditing is an independent, objective assurance and consulting activities designed to add value and improve an organization's operations."

The review starts from the perspective of the qualification and competence of the Internal Auditor, and then to the independency and objectivity of his functions that include risk assessment and management, and reporting to the appropriate authority. Independence requires that firstly, the internal auditor having helped to design the internal control structure does not get involved in financial transaction processes in the project, and secondly, that he is autonomous to the extent that his activities are not controlled by the internal mechanism of the operation of the project, and thirdly that he reports directly to the project governance body and/or the development agency.

The matter of internal auditor's reports is very important. The reviewer will check to see that it is regularly produced and submitted at the specified times, and that each contains observations and recommendations that are apt and poised to contributing to the effectiveness, efficiency and transparency necessary for accomplishing the project's objectives. Sequel to the submission of each report, it is also expected that the internal auditor follows up with the approving authority to obtain approval or otherwise of the recommendations made. If and how the internal auditor has ensured that the approved recommendations have been implemented by the project management team are part of the issues the reviewer will take note of.

External Audit

The audit of the Financial Statements of the project periodically (mostly annually) by an external auditor is usually one of the requirements of the Financing Agreement. The purpose of the external audit is to have the development agency and the project governance body informed by an external and independent auditor, of the trueness and reliability or otherwise of the financial statements presented to them by the project management team indicating the financial position of the project.

The act of external audit is an endogenous project-based system that continuously monitors the fiducial responsibility reposed on the project management team. Much that the reviewer of the financial management of the project with respect to external audit will do is to examine the engagement of the external auditors, the audit reports submitted by them and the reactions of the project management due to the audit.

Because of the sensitive role that the external auditor plays in the project, the process of his engagement by the project must be a concern to the reviewer. It must be seen to have been transparent and not had given opportunity for a compromise of the position. Attention is also paid to the tenure of the contract between the external auditors and the project. Tenure of three years is ideal in which case a maximum of consecutively three years of audits would have been carried out by the same auditor.

Examination of the external audit reports over the years is key to assessment of compliance to fiduciary requirements on the part of the project management team. Regularity and timely submissions of the reports to development agency and/or project governance body is considered here. For most development agency, they will for their projects require that the audit report of each year is submitted within six months after the end of the period covered by the report. This is to ensure that prevailing problems are dictated and reported early before the damage becomes severe.

On the content of the reports, though not generally reviewing the audit reports, the observations and recommendations made in the reports are focused on in the assessment with two intentions. Firstly is to find out whether the governance authority have upon receiving each of the reports paid sufficient attention to it as it deserves, reviewed the report, accepted or approved the recommendations or otherwise, or advised the project management team accordingly, or issued guidelines. Where none of these have been done, the audit report has been made not to serve its purpose. Secondly, the reviewer will want to see that corrective measures and steps in response to the observations and recommendations contained therein, or advice or approvals or guidelines issued have been diligently taken by the project management team. In this way, assurance of the project's discharge of its fiduciary duty is considered high.

Disbursement

As part of the assessment of financial management, the level of disbursements received by the project over the period spent is crucial. Primarily, the assessment involves the comparison between the actual disbursement received and the (1) actual works performed, and (2) planned disbursement. Where the disbursement received is significantly higher than the actual work performed, this may reflect inefficient management of the cash flow since the project is operating with idle funds. This not only is likely to increase the finance cost but pose a temptation for conversion of the excess funds to other uses.

On the other hand, when the disbursement withdrawal is lower than the planned disbursement over the period, it is also a concern to the reviewer. Some of the inferences that may be made against the project management team when there is low or delayed disbursement include:

- Unpreparedness in meeting the conditions for effectiveness;
- Poor planning, procurement implementation, or improper fund flow arrangement;
- Lack of technical capacity to make requests for withdrawals;
- Slippages in the project implementation;
- Low liquidity which likely will stifle the progress of the project;

- Inefficient use of the funds;
- Likely extension of the project completion period leading to higher cost of the project;

Counterpart Fund

Directly related to the disbursement is the release of counterpart funds to the project where applicable. A measure of the difference between the planned and actual will be considered by the reviewer. The implication of a delayed release is the same with delayed disbursement. However, additional consideration is given by the reviewer to counterpart fund in view of the inherent risks that include political, bureaucratic, and funds availability.

Procurement and Contract Management

The handling and results of procurement and contract management under the project are strong indications of the fulfillment or otherwise of the fiduciary responsibility on the part of the project management team. In this regard, test of compliance to fiduciary requirements will include the assessment of procurement and contract management. Although the reviewer may not go through the whole extent of procurement audit, but serious attention would be paid to the following to ascertain an assurance that the required fiduciary duty is in a positive course:

- Procurement Technical Capacity;
- Contract Procurement's Time Performance;
- Contract Procurement's Effectiveness, Economy,

Efficiency, Transparency, Fairness and Integrity; and
- Contract Management

Procurement Technical Capacity
The failure or success of procurement of contracts most depends on the ability to conduct the procurement process. Therefore, the reviewer's first check will be on the technical capacity of the project management team to drive the required procurement activities under the project. This will involve matching the responsible team member's qualification and experience with the nature, type and complexity of both the procurement procedures and activities, and subject of the contracts. For instance, an economist leading the procurement team will not successfully undertake the preparation of bidding documents, evaluation reports and contract documents for a building construction contract. A Quantity Surveyor would be a better professional to do that.

Contract Procurement's Time Performance
Contract procurement in a large and multifaceted project is the primary driver of the project. Therefore, time performance of the contract procurements is critical to the performance of the project. Normally, the procurement plan will provide the duration of the various activities in each of the procurement processes up to the conclusion of the award of contracts. The level of adherence to this plan always will be a concern to the reviewer as he understands that unfavorable slippages will result to adverse impact on the project that may include delayed completion and cost overrun.

Contract Procurement's Effectiveness, Economy, Efficiency, Transparency, Fairness and Integrity

As always, the objective of contract procurement in all projects is to obtain the appropriate Goods, Works, Services for the required purpose, at the required time and place, and for an appropriate cost. In this way, 'value for money' entailing effective, efficient, and economic use of resources is achieved in the course of meeting the project's objectives. Therefore, the reviewer will focus on each of the concluded or on-going contract procurement processes as per the associated:

- ***Effectiveness***

Effectiveness considers the contribution of the procurement process towards the accomplishment of the project objectives with respect to institutional or national economic, social, environmental development.

- ***Economy and Efficiency***

While economy is that measure of pricing of goods, works and/or services that expend the minimum quantum of resources to obtain an agreed level of output, efficiency relates to the process management and value of the input leading to the agreed level of output.

- ***Transparency***

Transparency requires that relevant procurement information is made publicly available to all interested parties, consistently and in a timely manner, through readily accessible and widely available sources at reasonable or no cost.

- ***Fairness***

Fairness is encapsulated in equal opportunity to and equal treatment of interested business seekers. Equal opportunity includes access to information and disclosure of evaluation criteria, terms and conditions of contract.

- ***Integrity***

Integrity entails absolute respect and commitment to one's obligations and promises under the project, and most importantly to uphold at all times the project and public interests above personal and undue interest of any other.

Contract Management

The purpose of contract management is to create and maintain a drive leading to each party engaging its equipment, personnel and expertise effectively and efficiently and in compliance with agreed manner and conditions deliver the expected results of the contract. How and to what extent this is achieved impact on the accomplishment of the project development objectives.

Therefore, issues of implementation of each of the contracts, particularly the payments under the projects will be of special interest to the reviewer. Upon an analysis of the information contained in a Contract Register that the reviewer expects to receive from the project management team, he will form an opinion and ascertain level of assurance of the protection of the project resources. A typical Contract Register is shown in *Table 27*. Project management software that enhances tracking of on-going contracts can be used to generate similar Table. Issues that may draw the reviewer's attention with regards to each contract from the analysis include:

- Process of the approval of the contracts;
- Validity and activeness of all the financial instruments;
- Unfavorable changes to the contract price and or completion period;
- Process followed in admitting the unfavorable changes to the contract;
- Delayed amortization of Advance Payment;
- Delayed payments on certified invoice; and
- Unfavorable Estimated Cost at Completion.

Table 27: Contract Register (*Turn at 90°*)

S/N	Contract Title	Procurement Method	Procurement Period	Award Date	Completion Date		Contract Price			Performance Security		Insurance		Advance Payment Guarantee		Advance Payment	Cumulative AP Repayment	Cumulative Certified Work (Invoice)	Cumulative Payment	Retention	Limit of Retention	Outstanding Payments on Invoice	Outstanding Value of Work
					Initial	Revised	Initial	Revised	Estimated Cost at Completion	Issuance Date	Expiring Date	Issuance Date	Expiring Date	Issuance Date	Expiring Date								
1																							
2																							
3																							
4																							
5																							

Project Management Reports

Project management reports produced by the project management team and submitted to those who supervise and exercise oversight function on the project is a show of commitment towards the assurance that there exists appropriate utilization of the funds or same is being judiciously pursued. Therefore, this report does matter to the reviewer.

The first aspect to check is whether the report is being submitted regularly and at such a period interval that the information contained therein will be useful for decisions to improve performance of the project going forward and not obsolete. For instance, for some projects, annual submission will be too long a period to effectively monitor and help the project, instead, quarterly will be most desirable. The second is the scope of the report. A typical project management report, particularly for World Bank projects will have three sections namely, financial report, progress report and procurement management report. Financial report will cover issues of disbursement, uses of funds, special accounts and cash forecast. Progress report will reveal the outputs by project activities and the related management issues enabling the output such as contract management. Procurement management report centers on the procurement process monitoring and contract expenditures.

Just as with audit report, the reviewer will examine predominantly how the project management reports have helped in regularly improving the discharge of fiducial responsibility of the project management team due to guidance or advice provided by project governance upon review of the reports.

Records Management

Records management particularly those in connection with transactions are essential for prove of fiducial responsibility. It does not matter the form the records may be - physical or computerized or online, all that the review wants to see is that they are provided and stored in such a way that it facilitates internal control, accounting and reporting, and most importantly auditing.

To begin with, it is expected that there exist policies and procedures dealing with the issues of creation, classification, preservation and disposal of records. The reviewer will check how these policies and procedures are observed and note if indeed:

- trailing of transactions are easily possible due to good classification of records;
- records are properly safeguarded;
- there is back-up system for computerized records;
- records are not exposed to risks of fire and the likes; and
- access to records is easily and exclusively available to those authorized.

Anti-Corruption

Although the reviewer is not an investigator, he will in the course of the assessment observe any abnormality in connection with the use of the funds from the perspective of whatever portends corrupt, fraudulent, collusive or coercive practice on the part anyone directly or indirectly involved in the project. The World Bank in its guidelines on preventing and combating fraud and corruption defines these practices as follows:

A "corrupt practice" is the offering, giving, receiving or soliciting, directly or indirectly, of anything of value to influence improperly the actions of another party.

A "fraudulent practice" is any act or omission, including a misrepresentation, that knowingly or recklessly misleads, or attempts to mislead, a party to obtain a financial or other benefit or to avoid an obligation.

A "collusive practice" is an arrangement between two or more parties designed to achieve an improper purpose, including to influence improperly the actions of another party.

A "coercive practice" is impairing or harming, or threatening to impair or harm, directly or indirectly, any party or the property of the party to influence improperly the actions of a party.

(World Bank, 2006)

The dangers of the occurrence of fraud and corruption in projects are enormous. For those projects funded by the development agencies, the result may include that:

- Funds are wrongfully diverted and not used or employed maximally for the purpose for which the funds were provided;
- The development objectives of the project are undermined;
- The funding of the project by the development agency is suspended or terminated;
- Sanctions including suspension of the participation in the development agency's funded projects are imposed on liable individuals, entities or country.

The concern of the reviewer in assessing compliance to the

fiduciary duty of the project management team is to see that there are structures in place that do not create opportunities for, but dissuade and prevent fraud and corruption, and ensure that funds received are used for the established purpose. Additionally, it will interest the reviewer to observe that despite the preventative and control structure in place, where there was a substantial suspicion or allegation or proven matter of fraud and corruption, the management had taken among others some of these actions:

i. Immediate reporting to the appropriate authority;
ii. Cooperation with investigating entities and granting of full access to records;
iii. Demand for restitution of affected resources from the confirmed perpetrators; and
iv. Termination of the engagement or participation of the confirmed perpetrators from the project.

Above all, the highest measure of compliance to fiducial responsibility is where impeccable standard of ethics is observed in the implementation and governance of the project with particular reference to procurements, contract administration and financial management.

CHAPTER FIVE

RISK AUDIT

Risk Management is one aspect of the project management that both the Performance Auditors and Financial Auditors will show high level of interest in during the conduct of audits. While the Financial Auditors will be more concerned with the risks revolving around active financial accounting cycle of income, expenditure and value, the Performance Auditor will want to have a complete view of risks in connection with all aspects of the project and the impacts on the project performance and achievement of the project objectives. Obviously to do these, the Financial Auditor will be focusing predominantly on the existing internal control and the Performance Auditor, on the availability and operation of risk management process.

Understanding Risks

Risk can be categorized into two - systematic risks and non-systematic risks. Systematic risks also termed as 'non-diversifiable risks' are such that one cannot influence or escape them. These include inflation, interest rate, political, market and government policy risks; natural calamities and war. Non-systematic risks on the other hand are such that a rational person has a choice of avoiding or otherwise. Both can be strategically managed. Therefore, the Auditor expects nothing less from the Project Management Team.

To understand risks in the context of project management, one needs to carefully consider the various definitions of risks that have been provided by relevant institutions and authors. The Association of Project Management and Project Management Institute simply regard risk as "causes of an effect on project performance". **Kerzner, 2017** defines risk as "a measure of the probability and consequence of not achieving a defined project goal" while **Nelewaik and Mills, 2017** see risk as "the chance or hazard of a loss, often commercial". Actually, to grasp the concept of risk in the project, it is pertinent to ponder the following questions: Is there a perceived event that may cause a deviation from the project performance? Is this event likely to occur? What is the strength of the likelihood? Should the event occur, what would be the resultant margin of deviation from the project performance? Project performance here includes cost, schedule, quality, social and environmental. The first question prompts what may be considered as risk while the other questions provide a lea way to the risk management. Combining both, Charpman and Ward, 2010 define risk as:

> *the implications of uncertainty about the level of performance achievable, portrayed by adverse variability relative to expected outcomes, assessed for each performance attribute using comparative cumulative probability distributions when measurement is appropriate.*

Tolerance and Rating of Risks

Whether a risk is significant to a project or not is a function of the probability of the occurrence of that event and the recognizable impact the occurrence makes on the project.

At the point of the consideration of what constitutes a risk, probability factor as well as impact level are assigned to the occurrence of the event by the Project Manager and his team and this goes a long way to determine how risks are generally considered and treated in the project particularly when the assignment is qualitatively done. As seen from uncertainty avoidance index, different project managers have different risk tolerance. Some by nature or culture are risk averter, risk neutral or risk seeker. A risk averter is highly sensitive to uncertainty to the extent that higher protection is required for him to accept risk. A risk seeker is less sensitive to uncertainty and more bullish to the point of being prepared to pay a penalty to take a risk. The one that is risk neutral is constant in his approach and recognizes neither incentives nor disincentives to take risks. These attributes affect the probability and impacts the project manager considers for a risk and further determine his rating of the risk as follows with respect to its effect on the project: very high, high, medium, low or very low. These rating are further dependent on the project manager's prioritization of project performance in terms of cost, schedule and quality.

Efficient and Effective Risk Management

Irrespective of the project manager's risk idiosyncrasy, what matter most to the Auditors are how sound the judgments of the project management team have been and the reasonability of the tools they have employed to search, identify and manage the risks. Strongly speaking, the audit is centered on whether the conduct of the project manager and his team has reflected efficient and effective management of the risks properly associated with the project. Effective risk management according to **Chapman and Ward, 2017** involves '*doing the right things with respect to the risk management process so that the project is risk efficient in the corporate sense and all other project objectives are achieved*'. It is about doing the right things as is sensible around the project base or contingency plans to continuously maintain on the project risk efficiency as such to have variability relative to expected outcome tend to optimal.

Efficient risk management here requires that both threats and opportunities possibly incidental to the project get the project manager's attention as to not only reducing underperformance but enabling excess performance of the project. On a narrow note and most importantly though, the totality of risk management with regard to project management is an act that involves planning for risks and the diagnosis of what may go wrong or fall short of expected; it entails the identification of risks, analyzing risks qualitatively or quantitatively, developing response strategies and implementing or controlling same accordingly. The practice should be seen as not being crises management, instead, a continuous and deliberate efforts towards preventing potential issues that may later become a problem and adversely impact the realization of the project objectives as planned. It is acting to ensure that nothing go wrong and if it must, it should not be much of a surprise and that the structure or response strategy are in place to avert or ameliorate the adverse impact of the occurrence on the expected output and outcomes of the project.

Aimed at installing early warning mechanism, containing risk events and increasing the measure of certainty of the project success, effective risk management places the project manager in a position that he is not reactive but proactive at every stage of the project life cycle. Stages of project life cycle include conceptualization, planning, implementation and completion of the project.

Risk Management Document

How the project manager has fared in the management of the project risk in more than any other way is first evidenced by the risks related documents created and operational at the project. By intuition, the auditors will reach out for these documents and predominantly base their review or assessment of the project in terms of risk management on the operations of the documents. These documents which usually are living (having the base and updates) and deliverables of Risk Management Process (RMP) include:

- Risk Register:

This is a collection of all the risks identified on the projects. Some of the information relating to the identified risks contained in the Risk Register are:

- Description of the risks;
- Causes and effects of events constituting the risks;
- Stage of the Project Life Cycle to which the risk is associated with;
- Area of project performance subject to impact;
- Estimated values of risks and potential impacts; and
- Status of risks.

- Risk Assessment Report:

This report provides, for the risks identified, the details of the analysis leading to the categorization of the risks into very high,

high, medium, low or very low and also the prioritization of the risks. The assumptions and justifications are also indicated in this document as part of the risk analysis.

- Risk Mitigation Plan:

This is a document constituting not only actionable strategies for the management of the identified risks but a clear risk-related roadmap that helps the project team along its way towards accomplishing the project objectives. It is a documentation of risks' probable occurrence, impact and strategy of response, monitor and control. The content includes the following:
  - Purpose and objective of risk management;
  - Rules for rating risks and performing risk management;
  - Actions required in respect of risks;
  - Timing of the actions;
  - Allocation of ownership and responsibilities to risk management actions;
  - Assignment of resources (including technical expertise) for risk management;
  - Established monitoring and control metrics;
  - Communication and reporting process;
  - Capacity building.

- Lessons Learned Log:

The Log is based on properly documented risk planning, occurrence of risks or otherwise, risk management strategy adopted and realized risk impact on performance. Lessons learned are collated not only for refining the plans and decisions going forward on the project but to form the basis of risk management of future projects and the organizational risk management.

RISK MANAGEMENT PROCESS (RMP)

The entire test of existence or the level or effectiveness and efficiency of risk management in the project is anchored on the established risk management process or otherwise. Risk management process is the formal process of risk management ranging from identification of risks to monitoring and controlling of risks from inception to completion of the project as practiced by the project manager and his team. It is what gives rise to the risk management documents mentioned above and most importantly, guides decisions on the risk management strategy to avoid, accept, control or transfer a risk per time.

It is not enough that the Auditors see the risk management documents presented, it would be of interest to them to have a quick check on the creation, adoption and operationalization of these documents. In this way, they will confirm the truism of the risk management culture and express an opinion on the performance of risk management necessary to achieve the cost, schedule and quality expectations of the project.

Creation of Risk Management Process

The process of risk management starts with making sure that the key questions endogenous and exogenous to the project are asked and addressed with high level of reasonability. These questions, process of providing answers to the questions, answers to the questions, and purposeful reactions to the answers when developed as a practice creates risk management process and culminate to the project's risk management. Best practice requires that the act, also documented begins at the early stage of the project life cycle and continues to the closure.

A simple framework of the process consists risk assessment, risk analysis, and mitigation. This can be detailed more into acts that involve:

- Identifying risks;
- Performing risk analysis;
- Planning risk response; and
- Monitoring and controlling risks.

The most comprehensive risk management process has been developed by **Chapman and Ward, 2017** in what they term SHAMPU - Shape, Harness and Manage project uncertainties. If this process is seen in any project, the Auditors would have no doubt that real and appropriate attention has been given to risk management by the project team. The framework of this process consists of many steps of which the specific activities in some of the key ones are summarized below.

Step 1: Define the Project

This is the start of the process and it involves making clear the project for every member of the team to understand and be able to isolate the associated risks. The subjects requiring definitions with respect to the project include:

- Project Parties (Who?): The parties to the project - whether internal, external, regulators, agents, competitors, etc;
- Project Objectives (Why?): The objectives are stated with the inclusion of metrics of performance and priorities to cost, time and quality;
- Project Design (What?): This deals with the product of

project;

- Project Plans (How?): The activities necessary to achieve the project are outlined with the time schedule;
- Project Resources (Wherewithal): The resources including funds required to execute project and the sources and time of availability are considered here;
- Project Timing (When?): The milestone dates and completion date are indicated.

At the end of this step, the deliverable is a document unambiguously showing all aspects of the project as to provide to the team a shared understanding of the mission.

Step 2: Focus the Process

This involves major two stages comprising firstly, the definition of the risk management process (RMP) scope and secondly, planning the process. The activities and questions to resolve here include:

- Who are the ones to prepare the RMP?
- Indicate the real purpose of the RMP and take a position on the need or otherwise for the involving risk analysis in the RMP;
- Develop a plan for the RMP;
- Consider the cost of carrying out the RMP and select the appropriate model;
- Estimate how much time is required for the RMP preparation.

Step 3: Identify the Issues

According to the SHAMPU model, this stage of the RMP is

critical for effective and efficient risk management. It involves the identification of the sources of uncertainties and matching the associated possible responses accordingly. At the end of the exercise, a full understanding of the sources of uncertainties (risks) constituting threats (or opportunities) to the project as well as the most appropriate (or risk efficient) responses available to the project management team are reached and documented.

Step3.1: Shortlisting of Risks

This task of identification of issues and responses are fundamental, and covers very wide subjects affecting the project to the extent that the project manager cannot just sit down by himself and come up with the document. A team of variety of experts from the project team and beyond is required to brainstorm at this stage. The Auditor may want to see evidence of the workshop wherein the brainstorming took place. In order not to omit any source that will impact on the project (negatively or positively), and to have a comprehensive register of sources of uncertainties, Chris Chapman and Stephen Ward, 2004 have recommended that a pattern be followed such that with respect to the project performance criteria (time, cost, quality or any other) and the six 'Ws' (Why, Who, What, Whichway, Wherewithal, When), the associated sources are outlined. In this regard, *Table 28* indicates some of the key leadings to source identification. In practice these leadings are further dissected to a higher detail to capture all possible risks and appreciate the significance of each of the risks.

Table 28: Performance Criteria and Risk Source Identification

Performance Criteria and the Six 'Ws'	Leadings to Source Identification
Cost	Capital Cost; Life cycle cost.
Time	Normal; Emergency; Political.
Quality	Technical Performance; Function; Capacity
Who	Parties; Entities; Stakeholders; Competitors
Why	Motives
What	Designs; Specifications; Variations
Whichway	Project Activities
Wherewithal	Finance; Material; Labour; Plant
When	Time; Time in relation to the 'Ws'
Project Life Cycle	Conceptualization; Planning; Execution; Closure

Step3.2: Risk Response Options

Along with the identification of the risks are the potential responses to the risks. The response to each risk is better decided as they are being identified. However, the response option may change depending on the outcome of the quantitative analysis of the risk conducted later. At all times, the risk response strategy should be such that considers both the appropriateness of the response and the efficiency of the implementation approach. The generic response options are four in number and are as follows:

- Acceptance: The risk and its probable occurrence are acknowledged and provisions made to accommodate the impact if and when it occurs;
- Avoidance: As the risk and its impact when it occurs cannot be tolerated, the source of the risk to the project is eliminated or substituted with an alternative;
- Control: For the identified risk, measures are put in place to reduce the probability of the occurrence and/or the impact on the project;
- Transfer: For the identified risk, the burden of the likely impact on the project if and when it occurs is shared with or transferred to others who have accepted to undertake it.

In addition to the above, Chris Chapman and Stephen Ward, 2004 have provided variants to the options that include adjusting the project objectives; changing the assigned probability of occurrence and level of impact; acknowledging risk but choosing to do nothing about it; or by choice remaining ignorant of a risk.

Generally, the choice of the option of response is among other factors dependent on:

- Available information on the causes and the magnitude of the impact on the fundamentals of the project;
- Available alternatives or otherwise; and
- Endogenous or exogenous influence over the risk.

Complementary to the identification of and response to the risks are also the opportunities. The Auditors will be interested on how the project has treated the associated opportunities. The response options when an opportunity is identified may include: accepting to wait and take the benefits of the occurrence; enhancing the probability of the occurrence; exploiting the good of the occurrence; and sharing the benefits of the occurrence with others.

Step 4: Structure the Issues

'Structure the issue' is all about sorting the identified sources of uncertainty and responses in the order that reflects interactions in terms of causality, dependency or mutual exclusivity among these sources and responses. Mostly following the pattern of project activities, the output of this exercise is a diagram of source-response structure that shows the links between activities, sources and responses.

Step 5: Clarify Ownership

It is a good practice to, for every issue (source of uncertainty) identified, the ownership is allocated to one or group of persons, entities, or stakeholders involved in the project. These persons or entities may be those in the project, parent organization, agents, regulatory bodies, beneficiaries, etc. The ownership of an issue entails that the responsibility for the management of that issue and the consequences rest on the allottee. Therefore, care is taken to ensure that the one who has been allocated the ownership of the issue is such that is best suited and able to manage and/or bear the consequences of the issue as the case may be.

Step 6: Estimating Variability and Evaluating the Implication

This phase of the risk management process deals with the analysis of the risks. It involves the process of employing for an identified risk, a probability of occurrence and the consequences of occurrence to determine the risk's level indicating impact on the fundamentals of the project – cost, schedule and performance. The commonly used risks levels are: high risk; medium risk; and low risk. In the case of qualitative analysis, a typical method is the mapping of the levels of probability of occurrence to the consequences of occurrence using equal matrix, say, 3 x 3 to derive the risks that fall into high, medium or low levels. High risks are such risk that the product of the assigned probability of occurrence and severity of the impact falls within the established range classified as high for the risk. For example, on a severity scale of 1 -10 and established risk classifications of 1 – 4, 5 – 7, and 8 – 10 as low, medium and high respectively, *Table 29* shows the risk analysis of risk items A – F.

Table 29: Qualitative Risk Analysis

Risk Item	Probability	Severity	Product	Risk Classification
A	85%	7	5.95	Medium
B	85%	10	8.5	High
C	30%	7	2.1	Low
D	60%	9	5.4	Medium
E	80%	3	2.4	Low
F	90%	9	8.1	High

Based on the above, the risk items 'B' and 'F' need to be examined further to enable the selection of reasonable response option.

Supposing these risk items are in terms of cost and there is for item 'B' a probability of 85% that the cost from a base estimate of $60,000 will rise to a maximum of 20% increment, the maximum risk will be $15,000 [(60,000/1 - 0.2) - 60,000] while the expected net risk will be $12,750 (15,000 x 0.85). If the response option is to accept this risk, then provision will be made to finance this extra cost of $12,750. In the same manner, supposing the risk items are in term of schedule, and there is in the case of risk item 'D' a probability of 60% that the period of execution will be extended by maximum of 20 days from the base period of 60 days, the expected net risk of the extension of the activity will be 12 days.

This simple method may be considered less effective and efficient by the Auditors since both the assignment of the probability of occurrence and severities of impact are subjectively determined by the project team. However, it is better than no analysis at all. A more effective and efficient method is the quantitative risk analysis wherein numeric probability estimates are used.

Quantitative Risk Analysis of Schedule

For the risk analysis of schedule, the most often used quantitative methodology is the PERT (Probability Evaluation Review Technique). This involves, firstly, the establishment of work breakdown structure (schedule of activities) in a sequential order and the computation of baseline duration of each of the activities; secondly, the assignment of multiples of alternate duration ranging from most optimistic to most pessimistic for each of the activities; and finally, based on these information, the establishment of a critical path of the completion of the project and the ascertainment of the different probabilities of the completion periods at various confidence level. Advancement to this method is the use of Monte Carlo simulation which is a computer software program. As baseline and multiples of alternate duration periods and sequences are inputted based on the expertise and experience of the team regarding all the activities, the software evaluates by simulation models as many as 1000 scenarios. In this way a probability distribution of all possible outcomes is produced giving the management team the opportunity to make informed decisions with respect to probability of achieving different completion periods as against assuming a single duration for the project. Statements such as 'there is a 10% (20%, 50%,90%, etc.) probability the project will be completed in 150 days (165 days, 210 days, 295 days, etc.)' can be made with strong measure of certainty.

Quantitative Risk Analysis of Cost

The Monte Carlo simulation is also used for the quantitative risk analysis of cost. The steps are apparently similar to the quantitative risk analysis of schedule except that the duration is replaced with cost in the analysis. For each of the activities which may be represented in the bills of quantities, the baseline cost is first realistically estimated. A multiple of alternate costs ranging from optimistic minimum value to pessimistic maximum value are assigned to each of the cost element. All are then inputted in the program which carries out the simulation as before in models numbering up to 1000. This analysis provides probabilities for range of costs as such that the management team can make reliable decisions based on cost peaks and the associated probabilities. In this way rather than sticking to a single cost estimate, multiple estimates can be made dependent on varying probabilities. Therefore, statements such as 'there is a 10% (20%, 50%,90%, etc.) probability the project will cost $2,000,000 ($2,200,000, $2,600,000, $3,100,000, etc.)' can be made with strong measure of certainty.

Step 7: Harness the Plans

Following the earlier steps, by now the project management team would have had insight of what can go wrong, the measure of this wrong, the impact of the wrong on the project and magnitude of likely shift from the project performance due to these things going wrong. Also, the response options to what can go wrong and the respective bodies best suited to manage it would have been known. Therefore, what is now needed in the risk management process is to harness all the outcomes of the previous steps and develop an all-embracing documented project strategy including management tactics that aims at mitigating the risks. The output of this stage is a comprehensive Risk Assessment Report culminating to Risk Management Plan. The Plan consists of risks sources, evaluations and actionable activities scheduled for the purpose of monitoring and controlling risks towards zeroing divergence from the project performance. A typical template of a Risk Management Plan is shown in *Table 30.*

Table 30: Typical Risk Management Plan Format (*Turn at 90°*)

<table>
<tr><td colspan="4">Project Name:</td><td colspan="6"></td></tr>
<tr><td colspan="4">Project Objectives:</td><td colspan="6"></td></tr>
<tr><td colspan="4">Key Performance Indicators:</td><td colspan="6"></td></tr>
<tr><td colspan="4">Primary Project Outcomes:</td><td colspan="6"></td></tr>
<tr><td colspan="4">Primary Project Outputs:</td><td colspan="6"></td></tr>
<tr><td colspan="4"></td><td colspan="3">Original RMP Date:</td><td colspan="3">Last Updated RMP Date:</td></tr>
<tr><td colspan="10"></td></tr>
<tr><td rowspan="2">Risk ID</td><td rowspan="2">Risk</td><td rowspan="2">Risk Sources</td><td rowspan="2">Anticipated Occurrence Point on PLC[1]</td><td rowspan="2">Assigned Risk Level</td><td rowspan="2">Risk Analysis Methodology</td><td rowspan="2">Key Assumptions</td><td colspan="3">Mitigation</td></tr>
<tr><td>Action</td><td>Person/ Entity Responsible</td><td>Monitoring and Controls by:</td></tr>
<tr><td></td><td></td><td></td><td></td><td></td><td></td><td></td><td></td><td></td><td></td></tr>
<tr><td></td><td></td><td></td><td></td><td></td><td></td><td></td><td></td><td></td><td></td></tr>
<tr><td></td><td></td><td></td><td></td><td></td><td></td><td></td><td></td><td></td><td></td></tr>
<tr><td></td><td></td><td></td><td></td><td></td><td></td><td></td><td></td><td></td><td></td></tr>
</table>

[1] – Project Life Cycle

Adoption of Risk Management Process

Although the entire risk management process is full of iterations, there is a need to at some point of the project particularly early stage of the life cycle have the risk management process adopted. The adoption will require that beyond the project management team that has the plan shared among them, some approvals are obtained from relevant authorities. The essence of this is to empower members of the project management team and other stakeholders relevant to the project's risk mitigation to in due course act appropriately without unnecessary recourse to approving authorities. The Auditors will be interested to see the formal adoption of at least the initial Risk Management Plan or/and subsequent revisions.

Operationalization of Risk Management Process

The mistake that is common with most projects is that after the team may have successfully prepared the Risk Management Plan, the document is locked up in the cupboard rather than being made an operational and a living document. Under the SHAMPU risk management framework, four basic tasks are required to be maintained simultaneously once the project starts regarding the risk management process. These are:

- Manage planned actions;
- Roll action plans forward;
- Monitor and control; and
- Manage crises and be prepared to respond to disasters.

At the implementation stage of the risk management process, the plan becomes handy such that every member of the project team keeps his/her eyes down to first deeply understand the plan, observe what is going on and respond appropriately and promptly at any given time during the project life cycle. As what are required of every team member in respect of occurring uncertainties are well documented and well known to him/her, monitoring and control of the risks become everyone's job according to the assigned responsibilities.

Monitoring involves the steady observation of the potential divergence of realities from target, expected value and commitment estimates as established in the base plan. Gantt Chart is one of the traditional indicator systems that relays these observations and divergence. Other techniques of the indicator systems for the project are Earned Value (cost per schedule), Program Metrics, Schedule Performance Monitoring or Technical Performance Measurement. The process of reconciling this divergence demands the review and update of the plan to reflect a more predictable future as such that early proactive actions are taken to minimize the departure from the original plan or ensure an optimal trade-off of cost, time and other quality performance. Of importance to the Auditor is to note that the act of monitoring and controlling is not the act of solving existing problems but perceiving, estimating and mitigating future problems that may arise in the course of the project. In a more dynamic risk monitoring and control atmosphere, Josephs and Rubenstein, 2018 have recommended that a common online platform for 'Risk Action Plan' be set up to allow each of the team members at any time of foreseeing potential risk post same indicating the cause, effect and impact on the project, and proposed mitigations. 'Cause' is the current true condition that gives one concern for a probable future bad outcome. 'Effect' is the future bad outcome that is a possibility and will harm the project. 'Impact' is the measure of success of the project that will be in jeopardy if the concerned future bad outcome becomes a reality. Periodically (say monthly), upon due considerations by the management team during a meeting scheduled for the purpose, the collated entries in the Risk Action Plan platform serves as the basis for updating the Risk Management Plan and the Project Risk Register.

The real operationalization of risk management process is reflected by the Project Risk Register. At a glance, all risks ever identified on the project, the primary subjects of the risk impact, value of the risk, value of the potential impact, status of the risk and risk mitigation actions are seen in a typical Project Risk Register as shown in *Table 31* overleaf.

Table 31: Typical Project Risk Register (*Turn at 90°*)

Project Name:											
Project Objectives:											
Key Performance Indicators:											
Primary Project Outcomes:											
Primary Project Outputs:											
				Risk Management Plan Date:				Last Updated PRR Date:			
Risk ID	Risk	Subjects of Impact[1]	Probability of Occurrence	Assigned Risk Level[2]	Risk Priority Scale[3]	Maximum Estimated Risk Value[4]	Potential Risk Impact Value[5]	Mitigation			
								Action	Risk Owner	Action by:	Risk Status[6]

[1] – The project performance likely to be affected by the risk (cost, schedule, quality); | [2] – The risk classification in terms of significance – high, medium or low; | [3] – The risk classification in terms of experience of mitigation – Super-high (no one ever has successfully mitigated the risk); High (the team has never succeeded in mitigating the risk); Medium (the team has not always succeeded in mitigating the risk); Low (the team has regularly succeeded in mitigating the risk); | [4] – The estimated value of the risk on the project if the occurrence is certain; | [5] – The estimated value of the risk on the project if based on the assigned probability of occurrence; [6] – The current state of the risk – no longer in existence (cancelled); successfully mitigated (closed); mitigation action is in progress (on-going); mitigation actions not due (open); mitigation action is due but not started (outstanding).

CONCLUSION

The attention the project management team has given to risk management can mar or make the project. The Auditors know this fact and therefore will always focus on this aspect of the project management whenever they are carrying out both performance and financial audits of the project. They are aware of the many benefits of risk management throughout the life cycle of the project. These benefits according to **Ochieng, Price and More, 2017** include that:

- Project overruns (cost, time) are avoided;
- Required quality and operational standard of the project are achieved;
- Commitment to monitoring and control become the norm;
- Potential crises in the project are eliminated;
- Innovation is encouraged.

On the other hand, the absence or shabby practice of risk management is a lead way to disaster that no project management team will wish that the Auditors confirm that they are exactly treading upon. Rather it will be better they say to the Auditor, in this regard, 'we have no spot.'

CHAPTER SIX

GOVERNANCE AUDIT

Governance refers to the process whereby elements in society wield power and authority, and influence and enact policies and decisions concerning public life, and economic and social development. (http://www.gdrc.org/u-gov/governance-define.html). In a more simpler form, according to **UNESCAP, 2009**, "governance" means: *the process of decision-making and the process by which decisions are implemented (or not implemented)*. The concept of governance can be applied in different context that includes national governance, corporate governance, project governance, etc.

In reviewing a project, governance of the project is a major aspect of the project that usually will have Auditor's scrutiny. Therefore, it is important that the project management team understands the issues of project governance in order not only to be able to respond to the demands of the governance but catalyze the governance entity in functioning to fulfill its responsibilities for the good of the project.

Project Governance

Project governance is a wide subject but for the purpose of this book should be understood from the classifications of organizational independence or domiciliation of the project to which the governance applies. Examining the different literatures, **Bekker, 2015** has identified the approaches along three different 'schools of thought' in defining project governance based on the classifications. These 'schools of thought' are single-firm school, multi-firm school and large capital school. The single-firm school is applicable where the project is part and not independent of the organization where it is domiciled. The operation is ruled by the internal mechanism of the organization in which case the project governance is exercised within the structure of the organization and involves the control, management, supervision and monitoring of the project by the organization's management. The extent of governance here extends to strategic and technical level of the project. Multi-firm school applies where there are two or more organizations participating in the project in which case the project governance is as in single-firm in terms of involvement and levels but covers the participating organizations. The rallying point of the project governance here are the issues of relationships, agreement, collaborations and contracts among the organizations. The large capital school is where the project is considered a temporary organization. In this case the project governance mechanism is external to the project and rather than descending to the technical level of the project covers strategic and institutional levels including external and macro environment affecting the project. Here, the project governance concentrates and deals with *politics, policy, principles, guidelines, decision-making, socio-economics, front-end, external stakeholders' interest, ethics, etc* (**Bekker, 2015**).

For the projects supported by the development agencies that this book is centered on, it is the large capital school of thought that applies. This is in view that in the implementation of most development agencies' supported projects, Project Implementation Units are established which are fully or quasi-independent of other organizations. Therefore, the discussion of project governance would be limited to large capital projects.

Characteristics of Project Governance

Where a project is considered as a temporary organization, the characteristics and principles of project governance are similar to that of corporate governance except that they are uniquely applied to projects. Since much is known about corporate governance, the principles of project governance are understood based on that of corporate governance as provided by **OECD, 2015** though **Bekker, 2015** has made some distinctions among the two in terms of the context (see Table 32, **Bekker, 2015**).

Table 32: Corporate governance in the context of projects

S/N	OECD's Corporate Governance Principles	Project Governance Context
1	Ensuring the basis for an effective corporate governance framework	Basis for effective project governance framework
2	The rights and equitable treatment of shareholders and key ownership functions	The rights of project financiers; Equitable treatment of all role players including implementing agency, contractors, suppliers, consultants, beneficiaries, etc

3	Institutional investors, stock markets, and other intermediaries	The rights of co-financiers and group interests and protection of social contracts
4	The role of stakeholders in corporate governance	Socio-economic and environmental care
5	Disclosure and transparency	Ethical conduct
6	The responsibilities of the board	Responsibilities of the Project Steering Committee.

Generally, as opposed to management and controlling the project, project governance in line with corporate governance concerns itself with the following areas in order to have the project meet the desired objectives (**Goergen et al, 2010**):

- Roles and responsibilities
- Accountability
- Disclosure and transparency
- Risk management and control
- Decision making
- Ethics
- Performance and effectiveness
- Implementation of strategy

Good project governance follows after generally acknowledged good governance which according to **UNDP, 1997** has eight characteristics. These good governance characteristics, also patterned after projects are as follows:

- **Participation**

Participation by all stakeholders in the project is essential for good governance. Not only are the interests of the different stakeholders a concern, there is a representation of the stakeholders in the decision-making process as regards the project.

- **Rule of law**

Good governance requires fair legal frameworks that are enforced impartially. The project documents, contracts and extant laws are essentials here.

Figure 13: Characteristics of good governance

- **Transparency**

Transparency means that decisions taken and their enforcement are done in a manner that follows rules and regulations. It also means that information is freely available and directly accessible to those who will be affected by such decisions and their enforcement. It also means that enough information is provided and that it is provided in easily understandable forms and media.

- **Responsiveness**

Good governance requires that institutions and processes try to serve all stakeholders within a reasonable timeframe.

- **Consensus oriented**

There are several actors and as many view points. Good governance requires mediation of the different interests and is evidenced by broad and long-term minded decisions.

- **Equity and inclusiveness**

A society's well-being depends on ensuring that all its members feel that they have a stake in it and do not feel excluded from the mainstream of society. This requires all groups, but particularly the most vulnerable, have opportunities to improve or maintain their well-being.

- **Effectiveness and efficiency**

Good governance means that processes and institutions produce results that meet the needs of stakeholders while making the best use of resources at their disposal.

- **Accountability**

Accountability requires that those making the decisions are accountable to those that the decisions made or actions taken in respect of the decision may affect directly or indirectly. Accountability cannot be enforced without transparency and the rule of law.

Project Governance and Project Steering Committee

Just as the Board is responsible for governance of corporate organizations, the Steering Committee is for project governance. Actually, the word 'govern' means 'steer'. Most development agencies' funded projects will have a Steering Committee constituted for the governance of the project. The Project Steering Committee is the apex decision-making body for the project.

Purpose of the Steering Committee

The purpose of establishing Steering Committee is to complement and support the project at strategic and institutional level. While the project management team concentrates on the technical and operational aspects of the project, the Steering Committee focuses on the institutional level by providing the structure through which the objectives of the project are set, and determining the means of attaining these objectives; and also monitoring performance (**OECD, 2015**). The purpose of the Steering Committee is further to prevent costly, adverse and undesirable decisions from being made by the project management team.

Composition of the Steering Committee

The composition of the Steering Committee should be broad to have all the interests in connection with the project represented in the Committee. However, the representation should be done by persons with relevant competencies, who understand the project, have some knowledge of project management and can add value to the decision process. The selection of members, also, should be such that not only that the appointees fit into anticipated roles and responsibilities required, they are also available to undertake same for the effective and efficient functioning of the Committee. Above all, it will make more sense to appoint persons with relevant authority to influence the socio economic and environmental conditions for the project to stride. This is very critical to the project.

Functions of the Steering Committee

Generally, the Steering Committee's functions include:

- Making strategic decisions regarding the project;
- Providing policy guidance to the implementation of the project;
- Coordinating at institutional level the different participating organizations in the project;
- Defining expectations for the project management team in terms of accountability and performance;
- Developing processes and rules necessary for accomplishing the project's goals;
- Granting powers to the project management team and others where necessary;
- Continually assessing the progress made towards the

project goals and the timing;
- Monitoring and advising on the risks' reduction as the project progresses.

In more specific terms, among roles and responsibilities of the Steering Committee are:
- Review and approval or otherwise of the Work Plan and Budget of the project submitted to it by the project management team;
- Review of the Reports of the Internal Auditors and advising or directing the project management team on the recommendations contained therein;
- Review of the Reports of the External Auditors and advising or directing the project management team on the recommendations contained therein;
- Review of the Implementation Progress Reports received from the project management team and advising or directing accordingly.

Focus of the Auditor

The focus of the Auditor in assessing the performance of the Steering Committee would be based on exhibition of the characteristics of good governance and the fulfillment of the roles and responsibilities expressly assigned to the Steering Committee. It is expected that if the Committee plays its role very well, it will have positive impact on the performance of the project management team and the project at large. Therefore, the questions the auditor would be seeking to find the answers will include:
- Is the composition of the membership and the capacities

of the members right?

- Have the Committee done what they ought to have done?
- Were the things done well and in good time?
- Is there a system or acts that ensure that the intended result of what was done are realized?

As the key indicators of the workings of the Steering Committee are anchored on meetings held, approvals given, policies developed, and guidance provided, the auditor would focus on these matters.

Meetings are major means of the Committee exercising its functions and therefore must be taken seriously. Whether the meetings were held virtually or in-person, the auditor will like to know if they were held regularly as specified in the project document. Were there quorum-level attendance always and reasonable participation of members in the meetings held? And, are the minutes of the meetings properly documented? These are the issues the auditor would be concerned with regarding the meetings.

Among the approvals expected to be given by the Steering Committee to the project management team after due review are the Annual Work Plan and Budget. Given that the submissions of these documents were made in good time, the Auditor will check how much time it takes the Committee to carry out the review, respond or give its approval for implementation. Obviously, any delay in attending to the Work Plan and Budget sure will adversely affect the performance of the project. Other key approvals expected from the Steering Committee are in connection with the recommendations of the Internal and External Financial Auditors. How the Committee has taken the Audit Reports and actions taken would be considered as one of the measures of the Committee's performance.

Closely related to approvals are issues of policies and guidance. A check would be made on if the Steering Committee had, based on the information available to it – Work Plan, Budget, Audit Reports, Progress Report, etc, developed policies and/or offered guidance to the project management team or others for the improved implementation of the project. Has there been directives and mechanism for follow-up on the directives? The auditor would want to know.

In general, the process of decision-making and the process by which decisions are implemented (or not implemented) (**UNESCAP, 2015**) and how these are consistent with the characteristics of good governance are the primary focus of the Auditors. Overall, the assessment is on how the functioning of the Steering Committee is helping to advance the progress of the project. This also goes to say that what the Steering Committee is doing that they ought not to, are also very important to the Auditor. The Auditor is mindful that some of the actions or inactions of the Committee could be an obstacle to the progress or realization of the objectives of the project. For instance, if approvals are unjustifiably withheld or decisions are politically motivated, these could mar the project. Additionally, common act that can be inimical to true governance and injurious to the smooth implementation of the project is any attempt by the Steering Committee to micromanage project management team and the project. An example is where the Steering Committee gets involved in the procurement processes of the activities of the project. These acts of intrusion that does not allow the separation between governance and management are among those the Auditor would be interested to observe and report accordingly.

The Role of Project Management Team

The project management team does not have any role to play in the project governance except that it has to be concerned with the performance of the governance body, the Steering Committee, in executing its functions. This is because if the Steering Committee fails, there is high propensity for the project management team and the project to fail too.

With the aim of succeeding in the project, the project management team can find ways to support the Steering Committee and help make them function effectively. Some of these ways for the project management team which also may be subject of assessment by the Auditor include it's:

- Submission of Work Plan, Budget and Implementation Progress Report in good time to the Steering Committee;
- Facilitating the timely submission of Internal Financial Audit Report to the Steering Committee;
- Requesting for the Committee's opinion and directives following the recommendations of the Internal Auditor;
- Early commencement and conclusion of the procurement process for the engagement of External Auditors;
- Requesting for the Committee's opinion and directives following the recommendations of the External Auditor;
- Facilitation of the scheduling of Committee's meetings and early reminder to members;
- Request for clarifications on policies and guidelines where necessary;
- Request for guidance on matters beyond technical and operational levels. etc

REFERENCES

1. Association for Project Management (APM). (2019). Definition of Risk.
2. Bekker, M.C. (2015). Project Governance – The Definition and Leadership Dilemma. Procedia - Social and Behavioral Sciences.
3. Chapman, C. and Ward, S. (2003). Managing Project Risk and Uncertainty: A Constructively Simple Approach to Decision Making. John Wiley & Sons.
4. Chapman, C. and Ward, S. (2010). Project risk management: processes, techniques and insights. Wiley.
5. Chapman, C. and Ward, S. (2011). How to Manage Project Opportunity and Risk: Why Uncertainty Management Can Be the Key to Successful Project Management. 3rd ed. John Wiley & Sons.
6. Chapman, C. and Ward, S. (2017). Project Risk Management: Processes, Techniques and Insights. John Wiley & Sons.
7. Collier, P.M. (2009). Accounting for Managers. Butterworth-Heinemann.
8. Drucker, P.F. (1973). Management: Tasks, Responsibilities, Practices. New York: Harper & Row.
9. European Court of Auditors. (2017). Performance Audit

Manual.

10. Goergen, M., Mallin, C.A., Mitleton-Kelly, E., Al-Hawamdeh, A. and Chiu, I.H.Y. (2010) Corporate Governance and Complexity Theory.
11. Institute of Internal Auditors (IIA). (2017). International Standards for the Professional Practice of Internal Auditing.
12. Josephs, A. and Rubenstein, B. (2018). Risk Up Front: Managing Projects in a Complex World. Lioncrest Publishing.
13. Kerzner, H. (2017). Project Management: A Systems Approach to Planning, Scheduling, and Controlling. 12th ed. John Wiley & Sons.
14. Nalewaik, A. and Mills, A. (2017). Project Performance Review: Capturing the Value of Audit, Oversight, and Compliance for Project Success. Routledge.
15. Oberlender, G. D. (2014). Project Management for Engineering and Construction. McGraw-Hill Education.
16. Ochieng, E., Price, A. and Moore, D. (2017). Major Infrastructure Projects - Planning for Delivery. Palgrave.
17. OECD (2015), G20/OECD Principles of Corporate Governance, OECD Publishing, Paris, https://doi.org/10.1787/9789264236882-en.
18. Public Company Accounting Oversight Board (PCAOB). (n.d.). AU Section 319, Consideration of Internal Control in a Financial Statement Audit.
19. The Institute of Internal Auditors (IIA). (2017). International Standards for the Professional Practice of Internal Auditing.
20. Turner, J.R. (1992). The handbook of project-based

management. McGraw-Hill.
21. UNESCAP (2009) What is Good Governance? United Nations Economic and Social Commission for Asia and the Pacific.
22. UNDP (1997), Characteristics of good governance, http://www.gdrc.org/u-gov/governance-define.html
23. Wallace, W.A. (2005). Internal Control Guide. CCH Incorporated.
24. World Bank. (2006). Guidelines: Sanctions for Fraud and Corruption.

ABOUT THE AUTHOR

OSONDU JOSHUA ONWUZURUIGBO is a highly experienced project management professional with over 25 years of expertise in quantity surveying, project management, and institutional development in Nigeria and Africa.

He holds a B.Sc. in Quantity Surveying from Obafemi Awolowo University, Nigeria, M.Sc. in Finance from the University of Leicester, UK, and Certificate in 'Innovation for Economic Development' from the Harvard University's Kennedy School of Government, USA.

Osondu began his career in 1992 at El-Rufai and Partners, a leading consultancy firm in quantity surveying and project management, and later joined Costain (West Africa) Plc, a British Building and Civil Engineering Contractor firm based in Nigeria. Between 2004 and 2007, he served the then Minister of Federal Capital Territory (FCT), Abuja, as one of the technical assistants responsible for the monitoring of the FCT projects with annual turnover of about US$200million. Afterwards, he functioned between 2007 and 2019 as Contract Manager at Nelson Mandela Institution, Director of Multilateral Projects at African University of Science and Technology, Abuja, and Administrator of Regional Scholarship and Innovation Fund (RSIF) at the Association of African Universities, Accra, Ghana, all of where he led the management of numerous projects predominantly supported by International Development Agencies such as World Bank, African Development Bank, African Capacity Building Foundation, and others.

These projects at various times were subjected to financial audits and reviews by world top audit firms that include Deloitte, Ernst & Young, etc., but there was no time the outcome of the audit or review was adverse to attract any form of sanctions. Conversely, as an independent Consultant since 2019, Osondu has been undertaking review of many projects or providing specialist technical assistance to organizations among those that include PricewaterhouseCooper (PwC) and Committee on Impact Assessment of Tertiary Education Trust Fund engaged to carry out audit or review of projects. He is also a recognized MAPS Assessor. MAPS is a collective initiative of international organizations and development partners for the assessment of public procurement systems.

This book reflects all of these experiences shared for the benefits of both the project managers and reviewers as regards to best practices with respect to 'what to do' and 'what to look for', in the interest of the projects.

www.ingramcontent.com/pod-product-compliance
Lightning Source LLC
LaVergne TN
LVHW100520110826
845146LV00002B/712

* 9 7 8 9 7 8 6 8 5 7 4 9 7 *